D1491171

ST. THÉRÈSE OF LISIEUX
. . . with confidence and love

by Susan Helen Wallace, F.S.P.

Foreword by
*The Discalced Carmelite Nuns
of the Monastery of St. Joseph*
Terre Haute, Indiana

Pauline
BOOKS & MEDIA
Boston

Library of Congress Cataloging-in-Publication Data

Wallace, Susan Helen, 1940–

St. Thérèse of Lisieux— with confidence and love / by Susan
Helen Wallace ; foreword by the Discalced Carmelite Nuns of
the Monastery of St. Joseph, Terre Haute, Indiana.

p.   cm.

ISBN 0–8198–7007–2 (pbk.)

1. Thérèse, de Lisieux, Saint, 1873–1897.   2. Christian
saints—France—Lisieux—Biography.   I. Title.

BX4700.T4W29   1998

282′ .092—dc21

[B]   98–14384
                                                            CIP

Cover and inside photos: © Office Central de Lisieux

Printed and published in the U.S.A. by Pauline Books & Media,
50 Saint Pauls Avenue, Boston MA 02130-3491.

www.pauline.org

Pauline Books & Media is the publishing house of the Daughters of
St. Paul, an international congregation of women religious serving
the Church with the communications media.

2 3 4 5 6 7   06 05 04 03 02 01

Permissions

The author wishes to thank the following publishers for their kind reprint permissions:

Quotations from St. Thérèse's autobiography have been taken from *Story of a Soul, Third Edition*, translated by John Clarke, O.C.D. Copyright © 1975, 1976, 1996 by Washington Province of Discalced Carmelites, Inc. ICS Publications, 2131 Lincoln Road, N.E., Washington, D.C. 20002. U.S.A. Used with permission. All rights reserved.

All other direct quotations of St. Thérèse have been taken from *St. Thérèse of Lisieux: Her Last Conversations*, translated by John Clarke, O.C.D. Copyright © 1977 by Washington Province of Discalced Carmelites, Inc. and *The Poetry of St. Thérèse of Lisieux*, translated by Donald Kinney, O.C.D. Copyright © 1996 by Washington Province of Discalced Carmelites, Inc. ICS Publications, 2131 Lincoln Road, N. E., Washington, D.C. 20002. U.S.A. Used with permission. All rights reserved.

The Scripture quotations contained herein are from the *New Revised Standard Version Bible: Catholic Edition*, copyright © 1996 and 1989 by the Division of Christian Education of the National Council of Churches of Christ in the U.S.A. Used by permission. All rights reserved.

"A Prayer to Obtain the Spirit of St. Thérèse," by Bishop Patrick V. Ahern, D.D., on page 133 is used with permission.

Contents

PRAYERS IN HONOR OF ST. THÉRÈSE

Foreword

Since the death of St. Thérèse of the Child Jesus and the Holy Face one hundred years ago, countless biographies and studies of this cloistered Carmelite nun have been written. These books have influenced the lives of the people of many nations and creeds, opening to them a highway to holiness and union with God. It is a highway without complicated road maps, a direct route which leads to love for all members of God's family who are our companions on the road of life.

The last words Thérèse penciled in her autobiography— *"with confidence and love"*—form the subtitle of this new book about St. Thérèse. This brief but powerful phrase points out a path of hope for our world. St. Thérèse's witness of confidence and love is a gift to our "today," which can be directed especially to our youth who are searching for truth, goodness and a purpose in their lives. They need heroes and heroines among their peers, true friends who will not betray their trust. The role of St. Thérèse in their world of "today" has the capacity to be *peer pressure* at its best.

In recounting Thérèse's story, Sr. Susan Helen has captured the spirit of Carmel and expressed it in a simple style which makes it both attractive and real. This biography can and should be a source of encouragement to all who continue their search for the ultimate meaning of life and love.

The *little way of spiritual childhood* asks only for confidence in a loving Father who embraces all people regardless of their life situation or vocation. We all have to go to God accepting our faults and good qualities, our weaknesses and our strengths. The way of St. Thérèse does not require great or unusual achievements, but a simple disposition of the heart, ready to find God in every passing moment, and surrendering to him with trust in both light and shadow, joy and sorrow. It means to recognize him present in every situation and event, no matter how small or insignificant. It is Love alone that counts. As St. Thérèse exclaims: "He has no need of our works but only of our love.... Love, how well our heart is made for that!"

This new book makes this message clear and invites us all to go to God...with confidence and love.

Discalced Carmelite Nuns
Monastery of St. Joseph
Terre Haute, Indiana

A Note from the Author

Saints reflect the image of Jesus in their faces and bear the marks of his wounds on their souls. To imitate Christ in the time, location and circumstance in which we find ourselves can easily seem like something beyond our reach.

How do you define the saints? As people who *do* great things? Oftentimes they are, but before they do great things for God, they love Jesus totally. Love transforms people into saints. God's love is infinite. It is the Holy Spirit alive in the Trinity of Father, Son and Spirit. The love of Father and Son *is* the Holy Spirit. The Spirit's love in human beings is a transforming power. This love alone can transform people into saints. Love is the secret, the motivation. Through reflection and prayer, St. Thérèse of the Child Jesus, a young Carmelite nun, found this secret: "Oh! How sweet is the way of Love! How I want to apply myself to doing the will of God always with the greatest self-surrender!" *(Story of a Soul)*

Thérèse was born in the Martin family home at 36 Saint Blaise Street, Alençon, France, on January 2, 1873. She died around 7:20 P.M., on Thursday, September 30, 1897, at the Carmel in Lisieux, France. She was not quite twenty-five. She lived almost a quarter of a century and was buried on October 4, 1897, in a quiet town cemetery in

Lisieux. And that should have been all there was to it. Of course, the Carmelite prioress would write about Sister Thérèse for the archives and Masses would be said for the repose of her soul.

We ask ourselves: what happened to spread this young woman's fame around the world? What is the story behind the nun and the *power* behind the story?

St. Thérèse of Lisieux...with confidence and love, is a biography of Thérèse of the Child Jesus and the Holy Face, also known as the "Little Flower." As we read her story and hear her own interpretation of the power of God in her life, we will be challenged to find a message for ourselves. Thérèse will demonstrate what can happen when people give themselves over to God. Thérèse's God is the loving Father who picks her up when she cannot climb the steep hill of perfection. Thérèse's God is the Crucified One whose scarred hands reach out to embrace her. Thérèse's God is infinite love, the Holy Spirit who fills her soul with himself. Her story is more than a biography. It is a divine *takeover,* a magnificent conquest on the part of God.

Thérèse invites us to let God do for us what he did for her. She will manifest to us the truth of Scripture: "God is love" (1 Jn 4:8). This book is offered as an introduction to St. Thérèse and includes excerpts from her own writings and conversations. Quotations taken from her autobiography, *Story of a Soul,* are cited as *(Story)* in the text. All other quotes are from her *Last Conversations* and her poetry and are cited as *(Conversations)* and *(The Poetry of St. Thérèse of Lisieux).* Thérèse's *Story of a Soul* should be read and meditated. From there, numerous other books, audio and video tapes offer additional information and insights.

St. Thérèse has a word for all who come in contact with her. Above all, she wants to bring us to her loving God. She wants to teach us how to love and let ourselves be loved.

Susan Helen Wallace, F.S.P.

PART 1

"Those who wait for the Lord
shall renew their strength,
they shall mount up with wings like eagles,
they shall run and not be weary,
they shall walk and not grow faint"
Isaiah 40:31

1

Beginnings

Thérèse's Birth

Thursday, January 2, 1873 was cold and the sky a steel gray in Alençon, France. As night set in, the Martins kept their vigil. Zelie's baby was born at 11:30 P.M. The family clustered around the big double bed, their eyes riveted on the infant in Zelie's arms. Louis Martin leaned over and lightly stroked Zelie's hair. Her face was lined and tired-looking, but she was peaceful. Louis would be fifty years old that August; Zelie was forty-one. The little girl in her arms was to be their ninth and last child. Five of the Martin children lived. Three had died as infants; one, Helene, had died at the age of five.

Louis and Zelie had decided on what to name the baby: Marie Françoise Thérèse Martin. And the family would call her *Little Thérèse*.

Marie, Pauline, Léonie and Céline looked on and tried to be helpful. Their sister was robust, they thought, probably nearly eight pounds. But Mama had more experience and she guessed six pounds. Marie would be thirteen on February 22; Pauline would be twelve on September 7; Léonie, ten on June 3 and Céline, four on April 28. In between Léonie and Céline, Helene, Joseph-Louis and Joseph-Jean-Baptiste had not survived. Between Céline and Thérèse, had come Melanie-Thérèse who had also gone home to God.

Papa lifted the tiny child and secured the soft blanket around her. Thérèse rested easily on his heart. She slept peacefully unaware of the admiring glances and the bonds of love that surrounded her. Mr. Martin walked slowly, quietly around the room, rocking the baby. Papa was experienced at this and the girls watched with admiration. Mrs. Martin dozed off while Thérèse's sisters waited for Papa to tire so that they could hold their new sister too.

Louis and Zelie Martin

Louis Martin had been born on August 22, 1823 at Bordeaux, France, and was from a military family. He was quiet, gentle, organized and patient. He excelled at his watch-making trade because of his diligence and patience. He excelled in business because of his integrity. When he was twenty-two and single, Louis had considered a religious vocation. The life of a monk, honed by prayer, contemplation and work, had appealed to him. Because he had no Latin background, however, he was not accepted as a candidate for the monastery.

Alençon was a peaceful town, quiet for its population of 13,600, and small. Despite the smallness, Louis Martin and Zelie Guerin were not to meet for several years, nor marry until he was thirty-five and she twenty-seven. Both loved their Catholic faith and both had felt at one time in their adult lives a call to follow a religious vocation. Each had been advised against it: Louis for lack of education; Zelie for lack of health.

Zelie's childhood had been lonely, as she once reminded her brother Isidore Guerin. Their mother had spoiled Isidore and had treated Zelie harshly, something she lamented with sadness throughout her life. Zelie and Isidore's sister Elise became a Visitation nun, Zelie a lacemaker and Isidore a pharmacist.

The love and affection Zelie had received from her sister and brother helped her to bear up under the stern treatment of her parents. When Zelie married Louis Martin in the Church of Notre-Dame on July 13, 1858, a joy she had never known unfolded for her. She and Louis had so much in common and they were in love. For the first ten months they lived a celibate marriage by mutual consent. Then a priest helped them to reconsider and the Martins began having their children. The world can be grateful for the priest who successfully convinced the Martins to have their family. If he had not done so, we would have been deprived of St. Thérèse of Lisieux. Zelie and Louis were warm and affectionate with each other and with their children. Their home was joyful and their children were happy.

First Separation

Marie Françoise Thérèse was baptized on Saturday, January 4, when she was two days old. The oldest Martin child, Marie, was the baby's godmother. A few weeks later the baby developed intestinal difficulties. That situation leveled off, but when Thérèse was three months old, sickness struck again. Zelie said: "She is very bad and I have no hope whatsoever of saving her. The poor little thing suffers horribly since yesterday. It breaks your heart to see her" *(Story)*. Mrs. Martin realized that Thérèse needed nourishment and fresh country air. The family doctor recommended that Thérèse be given into the care of a wet nurse for as long as necessary.

Rose Taille was a hardy, healthy woman. She lived on a farm eight miles outside of Alençon, in Semalle. Little Thérèse shared the farm life of the Taille family from March 15 or 16, 1873, to April 2, 1874. The little girl grew and put on weight. Her curly hair, bleached by the sun, lent a healthy glow to her tanned complexion. Thérèse loved the flowers and animals. Mrs. Martin wrote: "Her nurse brings her out to the fields in a wheelbarrow, seated on top of a load of hay; she hardly ever cries. Little Rose says that one could hardly find a better child" *(Story)*.

When Thérèse returned home over a year later, the Martins welcomed her with joy and genuine excitement. Their baby was lively and playful. She was alert and her eyes sparkled with delight. She must have missed the Taille family for a while but the Martins showered so much affection on their fifteen-month-old that Thérèse was soon as contented as she had been on Rose's farm.

Céline and Thérèse through Mama's Eyes

Marie and Pauline attended the Visitation boarding school and lived there while classes were in session. Mrs. Martin's letters to Pauline give glimpses into the personality and temperament of her two youngest children. Thérèse will quote her mother's carefully preserved letters in chapter one of *Story of a Soul*. "In the story of my soul, up until my entrance into Carmel," she wrote, "I distinguish three separate periods. The first is not least fruitful in memories in spite of its short duration. It extends from the dawn of my reason until our dear mother's departure for heaven" *(Story)*.

Thérèse called Céline "the little companion of my childhood." The girls were three and a half years apart. From the time Thérèse returned from the Taille family, she and Céline were inseparable. The fifteen-month-old Thérèse looked up to Céline and the two would laugh and play. Thérèse tried to stand up. Mama could tell that the child would be walking soon.

On May 14, 1876, Mama wrote to Pauline: "My little Céline is drawn to the practice of virtue; it's part of her nature; she is candid and has a horror of evil. As for the little imp, one doesn't know how things will go, she is so small, so thoughtless! Her intelligence is superior to Céline's, but she's less gentle and has a stubborn streak in her that is almost invincible; when she says 'no' nothing can make her give in..." *(Story)*.

Mama also noticed that Thérèse, though younger, insisted with Céline on having her own way. Mama realized that Céline quickly gave in. In her December 5, 1875 letter to Pauline, Mama wrote of Thérèse, "I am obliged to correct this poor little baby who gets into frightful tantrums; when things don't go just right and according to her way of thinking, she rolls on the floor in desperation like one without any hope. There are times when it gets too much for her and she literally chokes. She is a nervous child, but she is very good, very intelligent, and remembers everything" *(Story)*.

Since Céline was older than Thérèse she had daily home classes with Marie. Pauline was still at boarding school. Little Thérèse felt left out and would begin to cry. That was more that Marie could bear so Thérèse came into the room too. She was given a comfortable chair and some busy work like cloth to sew or beads to thread. While Céline learned her lessons, her little sister was getting her needle tangled up in thread and the tears would start again. "Marie consoles her very quickly, threads the needle, and the poor little angel smiles through her tears," Mama wrote to Pauline *(Story)*.

As the years passed, Thérèse's love for Céline grew. "I remember that I really wasn't able to be without Céline," Thérèse recalled in her autobiography. When Thérèse was still too young to go to church on Sunday, Mama would go to another Mass and stay behind with Thérèse. The spirited little girl would wait eagerly for sounds of the family returning from Mass. Céline would often bring home blessed bread and the two children would have a prayer service made solemn with a Hail Mary and a sign of the cross. Once Céline could not bring home blessed bread. It was gone before she got to the table. "I don't have any," Céline explained. "Then make some," Thérèse commanded *(Story)*. Céline got a loaf of bread out of the cupboard, cut off a piece, prayed over the bread and then the two girls ate it.

One spiritual conversation of Thérèse and Céline was recorded in a letter of Mama. Céline asked Thérèse: "How is it that God can be present in a small host?" "That is not surprising, God is all-powerful." "What does all-powerful mean?" asked Céline. Thérèse's answer was prompt and sure: "It means he can do what he wants!" *(Story)*

"I Choose All!"

Léonie had been born on June 3, 1863. On May 10, 1877, just before Léonie's fourteenth birthday, Mama wrote to Pauline that Léonie realized she was growing up. She gathered up her childhood treasures: doll clothes, fancy materials and her doll resting on top of the basket. Céline and Thérèse eagerly eyed the basket as Léonie set it on the floor. "Here, my little sisters, *choose*," Léonie said. "I'm giving you all this." Thérèse continued in her *Story of a Soul*, "Céline stretched out her hand and took a little ball of wool which pleased her. After a moment's reflection, I stretched out mine saying: 'I choose all!' and I took the basket without further ceremony."

Thérèse remembered the incident vividly and as an adult religious was able to find in her reaction to the situation a response that would indicate how she would approach the whole of her life with God. "I understood...there were many degrees of perfection and each soul was free to respond to the advances of our Lord to do little or much for him, in a word, to *choose* among the sacrifices he was asking. Then, as in the days of my child-hood, I cried out: 'My God, I *choose all!*' I don't want to be a *saint* by *halves*, I'm not afraid to suffer for you, I fear only one thing: to keep my *own will;* so take it, for 'I *choose all*' that you will!" *(Story)*

Train Ride with Mama

Thérèse was just two years and two months old when she and Mama took the train to Le Mans, France. It was March 29, 1875. Mrs. Martin's destination was the Visitation convent where her sister, Sister Marie-Dosithee, was stationed. The story is recorded through the adult Thérèse's eyes, perhaps as she had heard Mama telling it later. Thérèse must have been excited to meet her aunt, the nun. Sister Marie-Dosithee gave her a little white toy mouse and a small basket of candy. Thérèse was happy to have candy to bring home to Céline. But when they were leaving, as Mama and Thérèse went down the convent steps, Thérèse's bouncing movements caused the candy to spill. Mama kept walking. Thérèse's whimpering turned into loud cries. Still Mrs. Martin did not seem to slow down or respond. Perhaps she didn't realize her child's plight, or she may have been in a hurry to catch the train. A two-year-old child would see only what a two-year-old was capable of seeing. And the details remain unanswered.

Thérèse and Papa: a Winning Relationship

Louis Martin's hair was graying and thinning. He looked continually more distinguished. Céline and Thérèse could have been his grandchildren. He enjoyed them so much, especially Thérèse. She would listen for the sound of Papa's key in the front door. When she heard the click—and she always did no matter where she was in the house—she came running. She led the welcome committee. She would call "Papa, Papa," and hug her delighted father. Then she would sit on his foot, pony-fashion, and ride Papa's shoe into the sitting room.

Mrs. Martin, busy about the house, would ask her husband in a light-hearted way why he spoiled Thérèse. Papa, shrugging his shoulders sheepishly, would reply, "Well, what do you expect? She's the queen!" *(Story)*

One time, however, Thérèse was in a different mood. She was having a lot of fun out in the garden. She was swinging higher and higher and feeling very independent. Papa walked down the garden path. "Come and kiss me, *little queen,*" he called gently. Thérèse's blond curls fluttered in the breeze as her swing kept pace with the rhythm in her ears. "Come and get the kiss yourself," she called flippantly. Mr. Martin was hurt. He quietly refused and walked in the house. Marie was there and overheard the incident. She stopped her little sister's swing and helped her to understand that her behavior was not right. She had answered Papa rudely and had hurt his feelings. The little girl was overcome with remorse. She began to cry loudly. Her sobs filled the big house and she climbed the steps without waiting for help. She found Papa and flooded him with affection. The little queen was quickly forgiven.

One thing stands out about Thérèse's earliest years: she was much wanted, much loved. She wrote: "God was pleased all through my life to surround me with love, and the first memories I have are stamped with smiles and the most tender caresses" *(Story)*.

2

Journey into Sorrow and Beyond

The first phase of young Thérèse's life was filled with joy and the fun of childhood. She was an infant when sickness had gripped her and her family bore the worry and pain. Now at the age of four, Thérèse would experience sorrow that she would never forget.

The cancerous tumor Zelie Martin had carried with her for several years was at that time considered inoperable. Mrs. Martin looked pale and dwarfed in her big bed. Thérèse and Céline sensed the tenseness in the faces of Papa, Marie, Pauline and Léonie. The two youngest knew they shouldn't talk. They stayed near Papa like little statues while the adults moved around them, taking care of Mrs. Martin's needs. The priest had administered the Anointing of the Sick while Mr. Martin's silent tears turned into sobs. Thérèse stayed near Papa and wanted to tell him not to cry. She wanted Jesus to make her mother well again, but Mrs. Martin only became sicker. In the early morning hours of August 28, 1877, the woman died. She was forty-six years old.

Thérèse could sense what death was because of the reaction of her family. She experienced a new emotion, a feeling of aloneness. She stayed near Papa and Céline, quiet and very alert. Papa would take care of things. Papa would know what to do. After a long time, the tears of the

Martin family ceased. Thérèse remembered distinctly standing quietly near her father next to her mother's coffin. Mr. Martin lifted Thérèse gently and said to his four-year-old: "Come, kiss your poor little mother for the last time" *(Story)*.

The day of Mrs. Martin's funeral her children were standing around silently. Louise Marais, who was the Martin's maid until the death of Zelie, said to the girls: "Poor little things, you have no mother any more!" *(Story)* Céline quickly asked Marie if she would be her mother now. Thérèse usually copied Céline's example, especially because her sister was three and a half years older. Thérèse hugged Pauline and cried: "Well, as for me, it's Pauline who will be my Mama!" *(Story)*

Les Buissonnets—The Little Bushes

The first phase of Thérèse's life concluded with the death of her mother when she was four. The second lasted from her mother's death until she was fourteen. The final period began with her entrance into Carmel at the age of fourteen and ended with her death at twenty-four.

Slowly the family continued their day-to-day living. The two older girls took over many of the responsibilities of managing the house and raising the smaller children. Thérèse idolized Marie and Pauline who brought so much love into her life. She said of her father, who had suffered more than anyone over the loss of his wife: "Our father's *very affectionate heart* seemed to be enriched now with a truly maternal life!" *(Story)* Despite the continued loving affection, little Thérèse became pensive and cried easily.

Louis Martin felt the weight of the loss of his wife. He began toying with the idea of relocating his family to Lisieux, about sixty miles away from Alençon. Zelie's brother, Isidore Guerin, owned the local pharmacy there. He and his wife were close relatives. They would be supportive and loving. Louis Martin esteemed Isidore as though the man were his own brother. The Guerin girls, Jeanne, nine, and Marie, seven, would be friends and schoolmates of the younger Martin girls.

On November 15, 1877, Papa Martin and his family said their good-byes to Alençon. Marie and Pauline felt the move deeply. It was hard to leave the friends, neighbors and favorite pastimes they had grown up with. The move, coming as it did so close to their mother's untimely death, was like another death. But Mr. Martin felt sure that his family would adjust well and quickly once they were settled in Lisieux. The carriage moved ahead. The driver reined the horses in front of the Guerin home. Uncle and Aunt Guerin were expecting them. Jeanne and Marie were at the door, eager to greet their relatives and bring them into their home to a hot meal and the warmth of the fire.

Thérèse was excited. Her eyes became bright and eager once again, as when Mama was alive. "I experienced no regret whatsoever at leaving Alençon," she wrote. "Children are fond of change, and it was with pleasure that I came to Lisieux" *(Story)*.

The next morning Uncle Guerin escorted his relatives to their new home. It was located in a quiet neighborhood, next to a park. The house had an English garden in the front yard and a vegetable garden in the back. It was spacious and ornate. Thérèse liked it, especially the well-lighted room at the top of the house called a *belvedere*. Mr. Martin soon lined the walls of the *belvedere* with books, making it his study. On bright days the warmth of the sun's rays penetrated the gray and the cold of winter. Thérèse would grow to love the *belvedere* especially because it was Papa's own domain. There he was *king* and his youngest daughter agily mounted the stairs at will for an audience with the "king of France and Navarre" *(Story)*.

The Martin's new home received its name—*Les*

Buissonnets (The Little Bushes)—because of the small bushes that bordered the front yard.

Life at *Les Buissonnets*

There was something mystifying about *Les Buissonnets.* Lively four-year-old Thérèse loved the security of the large spacious rooms where she could romp and play games with Céline. During those early years, Thérèse began to take home lessons from Marie and Pauline. Marie taught her writing and Pauline taught her catechism, sacred history and grammar. The youngest Martin liked her classes, especially catechism and sacred history, and she did well in those subjects. But grammar was another story. Thérèse wrote: "Grammar frequently caused me to shed many tears. You no doubt recall the trouble I had with the masculine and feminine genders!" *(Story)* But Thérèse's overall performance reflected dedication and a maturity beyond her years. She would climb the stairs to the *belvedere* at lunchtime to report the results of the classes to her king. Sometimes she had an award to show as she went over her grades with Papa. He would lift Thérèse onto his lap and hug her, calling her his *little queen.*

As the seasons changed and sunny days transformed the grounds of *Les Buissonnets* into a sea of flowers and grass and a thriving vegetable garden, Thérèse loved to play outdoors. Papa would come out to the backyard with his book or his paperwork and keep Thérèse and Céline company while they played. When Céline was at school with Léonie, Thérèse had Papa to herself. During the months when the weather was warm, father and daughter would take an afternoon walk. They would make a short pilgrimage to one of the nearby Catholic churches or a convent chapel to make their daily Eucharistic visit.

Thérèse vividly recalled the first time she and Papa prayed in the Carmelite chapel. Papa pointed to the grille, what looked like a strange wall of bars to Thérèse. Mr. Martin explained that the nuns lived behind the grille. Thérèse wrote later: "I was far from thinking at the time that nine years later I would be in their midst" *(Story)*. Father and daughter would walk home, hand in hand. Mr. Martin would usually buy Thérèse a treat and then she would do her homework. When her daily assignment was completed, she would resume her play in the garden. She loved to play tea party and mix her special brew of bark, seeds and water. Papa was her privileged guest at every tea party. She offered her concoction and Papa would pretend to be so pleased. Thérèse, of course, would pour some for herself as well. She and Papa would chat politely and pretend to drink their tea. When the social was over, he would ask softly out of the corner of his mouth if he should throw out the liquid. Thérèse occasionally directed that the mixture be thrown away, but usually she kept it in the hopes that there would be another tea party later that day.

Thérèse took care of the little backyard patch that was her garden. Papa took her fishing too. While Mr. Martin fished, Thérèse would usually sit quietly nearby in the grass amidst the wild flowers. She would think deep thoughts. She wrote: "Without knowing what it was to meditate, my soul was absorbed in real prayer. I listened to distant sounds, the murmuring of the wind, etc. At times, the indistinct notes of some military music reached me where I was, filling my heart with a sweet melancholy. Earth then seemed to be a place of exile and I could dream only of heaven" *(Story)*.

Lessons Not in Books

On a particular afternoon, when the sun's rays bathed Thérèse's face, she thought about God, her mother and heaven. She watched Papa fishing contentedly. She felt that Jesus was present in her whole being, that he knew

her personally and loved her personally the way Papa did
—only more because God is God.

The afternoon passed. It was time to eat the treats that
the child had brought from home for her father and her.
Pauline had prepared the food while Thérèse watched
with interest. Her sister had cut slices of freshly baked
bread and coated them generously with jam. Sitting on the
hillside now, Thérèse gazed down at the basket and remembered how the jam had glistened when the bread was
first prepared. She hoped that Papa was ready for his
snack because she was.

Mr. Martin put his fishing gear away and sat down next
to Thérèse. They said a prayer and then Thérèse opened
the basket. As an adult, she wrote of this incident to
Pauline: "The *beautiful* bread and jam you had prepared
had changed its appearance: instead of the lovely colors it
had earlier, I now saw only a light rosy tint and the bread
had become old and crumpled. Earth again seemed a sad
place and I understood that in heaven alone joy will be
without any clouds" *(Story)*.

Another afternoon, Papa fished and Thérèse enjoyed
looking at all the wild flowers while thinking about the
God who made them. Clouds suddenly rolled in and covered the sun like a shutter. Mr. Martin called Thérèse to
come as he hastily packed his fishing gear. The raindrops
grew bigger. Thunder rolled and lightning flashed. Mr.
Martin wanted to take the shortest way home. That would
take them through fields with grass taller than Thérèse.
Papa lifted his daughter onto his back, and picked up his
rod and bait. Then he walked swiftly, cutting through
several fields, until they arrived home. Although Papa
could hardly have agreed with her, Thérèse thought the
adventure was thrilling.

When Thérèse was six, she and Papa were distributing
alms as they did on a regular basis. Mr. Martin realized that

it is easy to admonish children to be grateful for what they have, to appreciate their blessings and to share cheerfully with the less fortunate. But he never preached with words. His quiet, continuous example was his sermon. His youngest child watched transfixed as Papa listened to the needs of one person after another. He gave money, helped people find jobs, made recommendations. Thérèse stayed close to him, hanging on every word.

As father and daughter were on one of their walks, an invalid on crutches dragged himself ahead. Thérèse felt his pain and frustration as he inched along the sidewalk. She slipped her hand out of Papa's and ran up to the man, holding out her one coin to him. That was all the money she had at the moment and she just wanted to share his burden, to lighten his pain. But the man did not accept the coin. He shook his head and smiled sadly as he continued on his way.

The little girl's heart ached. Perhaps he would like the small cake her father had just bought her a short while before. But she didn't want to hurt Papa's feelings either. Thérèse wanted to help the man and she suddenly realized how she could do it. "I remembered having heard that on our First Communion Day we can obtain whatever we ask for, and this thought greatly consoled me. Although I was only six years old at the time, I said: 'I'll pray for this poor man the day of my First Communion.' I kept my promise five years later..." *(Story)*.

Teasing and a Tantrum

In looking back over her youngest years, Thérèse recalled a certain May when she was still too young to attend evening devotions at church. She was left in the care of Victoire, a young woman who worked for the Martins. Victoire had a mischievous streak in her and occasionally liked to tease the younger girls, especially Thérèse. The

earnest little Thérèse wanted to conduct Marian devotions
on the May altar in her room. It was time for Thérèse and
Victoire to begin the prayers and hymns. But the older girl
kept teasing Thérèse. She wouldn't start the prayers. Instead, she just kept smiling, pretending not to hear
Thérèse's entreaties. The little child was baffled. She felt
the anger in her heart erupt as she pursed her lips and
stamped her feet. Her cheeks were flushed, her eyes blaz-
ing. Victoire was stunned. She had never seen such a
performance. Even while Thérèse shouted and stamped
her feet, she felt a flood of sorrow wash over her anger.
She was deeply repentant especially because Victoire had
brought her two little candle ends for the service as a
surprise. Victoire had gone overboard in her teasing, but
for little Thérèse, that was not the point. She had let her
temper run away with her.

First Confession

Thérèse knew that she did not want to offend God. In
fact, she wanted to grow in love for him. She was prepared
well for her first confession especially because Pauline had
explained that the priest took the place of Jesus in this
wonderful sacrament. Years later she wrote to Pauline, "I
made my confession in a great spirit of faith, even asking
you if I had to tell Father Ducellier I loved him with all my
heart as it was to God in person that I was speaking" *(Story)*.
Thérèse made her confession with confidence because
Pauline had told her that the tears of Jesus would purify
her soul.

Thérèse received the sacrament of Reconciliation before feast days "and it was truly a *feast* for me each time,"
she wrote *(Story)*.

Written in Heaven

Thérèse stored up happy memories of Sundays and feast days. Going to church as family, sharing meals, taking walks, being part of conversations and games, visiting relatives, saying evening prayer together—all of this deepened the realization of how much she was loved. Thérèse sat next to her father at Mass. She looked up at him frequently, especially during the sermon. She always listened intently to Father Ducellier although she could not really understand the meaning of the homilies. The first sermon she understood was on the passion of Jesus. It impressed her deeply and she never forgot it.

One Sunday evening as Papa and Thérèse walked home from Aunt and Uncle Guerin's home, Thérèse looked up at the stars. The night was clear and the little girl noticed that one cluster of stars was shaped like a "T." "I pointed them out to Papa and told him my name was written in heaven" *(Story)*.

Thérèse at eight with her sister, Céline, 1881.

3

Some Childhood Mysteries

Each member of Thérèse's family had a unique part to play in molding the girl's personality. Each also left warm memories of generosity and Christian witness. After Papa, no one was so dear to the *little queen* as Pauline. During the time before Pauline's entrance into Carmel, she was there for Thérèse to answer her questions or to care for her during childhood illnesses.

Thérèse recalls wondering about the saints. They were all so different, she reasoned. Some had led long, others short lives. Some had been martyrs; others had lived faithfully as ordinary Christians. What happened to them in heaven? Were some happier than others? If those who had performed greater accomplishments received a glorious reward, would the saints of *little deeds* receive less? If this were the case, how could they be happy? Pauline would know about such things, Thérèse decided. Her older sister sent her into the dining room to find Papa's large tumbler. Thérèse brought it back to Pauline who set it next to Thérèse's sewing thimble. Pauline filled both to the brim with water and asked her little sister to describe how full each was. Both receptacles were completely full. Pauline "helped me understand that in heaven God will grant his elect as much glory as they can take" *(Story)*.

Mysterious Visitor

In the joyful atmosphere of *Les Buissonnets*, Thérèse felt secure. The love of her family had helped her to find stability. Her sisters and her father grew in stature. Papa was her own king. One summer day in 1879 or 1880, Thérèse was sitting at a window looking out over the backyard of their home. The day was bright and she was enjoying the warmth and sunshine. She was alone in the attic room. Her two oldest sisters, Marie and Pauline, were together in a neighboring room. Mr. Martin had been away on a business trip for several days and was expected to return in two more days. Suddenly, a man dressed like Papa and of his same build appeared in the walled backyard. He walked like Papa, but something was strangely different. The man was old and stooped and moved slowly across the yard. Thérèse strained to get a good look. She realized that the man wore a covering like a veil over his face. His hat was just like Papa's.

The little girl instinctively began to call "Papa, Papa!" Fear gripped her. She felt confused. The mysterious visitor seemed not to hear. He continued to walk toward the grove of trees. Thérèse expected to see him emerge from the trees, but he never did. He had disappeared as silently as he had come. Thérèse was relieved when Marie and Pauline came running into the room. Marie had realized from her little sister's tone that something out of the ordinary was occurring, but she had remained calm, not wanting Thérèse to pick up on her own fear. The older girls took their little sister into the garden and examined the area carefully. The man was not there. Victoire insisted that she had not been involved in a prank. The incident was over, but it remained etched on Thérèse's soul. The meaning, what *was* the meaning?

Many years later, Thérèse and Marie, both Carmelite nuns, enjoyed conversation on a feast day in the monastery. The topic of Thérèse's vision many years before came up and the two sisters finally deciphered its meaning. Papa had suffered paralysis during the last five years of his life. The paralysis affected his mind. "Just as the adorable Face of Jesus was veiled during his passion, so the face of his faithful servant had to be veiled in the days of his sufferings in order that it might shine in the heavenly Fatherland...!" Thérèse said *(Story)*.

Other memories remained equally alive for Thérèse. She loved family vacations at the seashore. As she and Pauline sat on a large rock watching the sunset one time, Thérèse imagined herself to be like a small sailboat gliding confidently across the sea to heaven. "And near Pauline," she wrote, "I made the resolution never to wander far away from the glance of Jesus in order to travel peacefully toward the eternal shore" *(Story)*.

New Challenges

Thérèse was eight and a half when Léonie finished her studies at the Benedictine school. Thérèse began her classes there. Céline, three and a half years older, was a student there too. The youngest Martin girl did not adjust easily to her new environment. The close family life she had experienced and the security of being loved and accepted was all she had ever known. Now, Thérèse had neither Céline nor the Guerins to lend their support. A fellow classmate, an older girl who struggled in her studies, took a disliking to Thérèse, who was one of the youngest and brightest students in the class. "She experienced a jealousy pardonable in a student," Thérèse wrote. "She made me pay in a thousand ways for my little successes" *(Story)*.

Thérèse continued to study well. She often excelled because of the quality of her home classes with Marie and Pauline. Her two older sisters had laid the scholastic framework on which their youngest sister could build. But the child who had lost her mother at the age of four was not the outgoing, vibrant girl who once had amazed Mama. Thérèse had grown into a shy and sensitive young lady. She suffered when she was the butt of mean words or actions. She suffered especially because she did not know how to defend herself. She felt a sadness, an aloneness that she could not share with anyone except Jesus. She could be herself with him alone and she spoke to him in her heart. Thérèse's only relief and joy came when she and Céline walked home from school and the door of *Les Buissonnets* opened wide to them. Papa's warm welcome and interest in her scholastic progress helped her to focus on the many good things that filled her daily life. "I would jump up on Papa's lap, telling him about the marks they were giving me, and his kiss made me forget my troubles" *(Story)*.

Growing up was painful for Thérèse, particularly during the years from 1881 until 1883. She cried easily and seemed to find communicating awkward. But there were humorous moments, too. She and her cousin Marie played "hermits" and walked down a street with their eyes closed, pretending to be blind. They knocked over some cases placed at the entrance of a store. The shouts of an angry shopkeeper brought the two little girls quickly to their senses. Wide-eyed, they ran down the street.

Growing up with Céline was another joy for Thérèse. Once she had squirmed out of her highchair to follow Céline after supper, and their friendship continued to deepen. As children, Thérèse, though younger, had been the more aggressive. Now the two seemed to trade places. Céline was outgoing and Thérèse was the quiet one, often on the verge of tears. Céline defended her younger sister at school. She took care of Thérèse and played with her. They played school with their dolls. Céline being the leader directed the way the dolls would behave. Her dolls were quite good while Thérèse's dolls were naughty at times and the teacher had to dismiss them from the classroom. Thérèse was "Céline's little girl." But when the children had a disagreement, Céline sometimes became annoyed. "You're no longer my little girl," she would declare. "That's over with, and I'll *always remember it!" (Story)* Thérèse's tears brought an instant change of heart to the older girl and a reprieve for her little sister.

The two girls bought small gifts for each other, paid for, of course, by Papa. When Céline began preparing for her First Communion, Thérèse listened as Pauline instructed her each evening. The wonderful day grew closer. It was as if the two children were both making First Communion. Thérèse resolved to begin living a new life as if she too were receiving communion.

Pauline's Call to Carmel

Thérèse had once told Pauline of her desire to become a hermit. Pauline responded that she too wanted to be a hermit, then playfully promised to wait until her youngest sister was grown up so that they could go together. The sensitive child never forgot the promise. Then one day Thérèse overheard Pauline and Marie talking. Pauline was saying that she was entering the monastery. She would be joining the nuns at Carmel very soon. Thérèse was stunned. She understood what a *monastery* was. Papa had taken her to the Carmelite chapel. Together they had prayed to Jesus in the tabernacle. They had seen the grille and Mr. Martin had explained that the nuns lived behind that enclosure. On the one hand, the nuns' life was mysterious and inviting to Thérèse. On the other hand, it would require of the child a gift greater than she could give at that time in her life. Once, as a four-year-old, she had stood looking up at her mother's coffin. She had kissed her mother's forehead and clung to Papa's hand. Now she stared in her imagination at the monastery grille and imagined her precious Pauline, her second mother, disappearing behind it. "I did not yet understand the *joy* of sacrifice. I was *weak,* so *weak* that I consider it a great grace to have been able to support a trial that seemed to be far above my strength!" *(Story)*

Pauline patiently explained what her vocation to Carmel was and what it meant to her. It was not the building, or the nuns or the daily routine of prayer and work. It was a call from the Lord, an invitation to draw closer to him in a life of total consecration. Thérèse listened intently and thought about her conversation with Pauline. The girl turned the words over and over in her nine-year-old mind. She pictured religious life as a garden, like the well-kept backyard of *Les Buissonnets.* Close to nature, alive and fresh, this garden offered the environment for healthy flowers and plants to grow. Thérèse decided that she too would enter Carmel, not "for *Pauline's sake,* but for Jesus alone" *(Story).*

Pauline arranged for Thérèse to pay Mother Marie de Gonzague a visit at Carmel one Sunday afternoon. Thérèse was delighted to see the prioress in person and to be able to confide her desire to follow Jesus as a Carmelite. Marie Guerin accompanied her cousin, but each of the girls spoke privately with the prioress at Thérèse's request. Mother Marie de Gonzague told Thérèse that she had a vocation, but that she would have to wait until she was sixteen to begin her life in Carmel.

The Martins and Guerins were permitted to visit Pauline for a half hour weekly. Thérèse and Céline usually only had a few minutes with their older sister because time sped by. Thérèse began to have headaches. She suffered from insomnia. She became so sick that she was actually bedridden for two months. She was aware of the conversations and activity around her, but she could not respond. Mr. Martin had Masses celebrated at Our Lady of Victories in Paris. During the novena of Masses, Marie knelt and prayed before the family statue of Our Lady. "A miracle was necessary," Thérèse said many years later, "and it was Our Lady of Victories who worked it" *(Story)*.

Marie asked the Blessed Virgin to cure her little sister, to release her from the powers of darkness. Even as she prayed, Thérèse's eyes became riveted to the statue. The tormented girl saw a smile form on the Virgin's face. Suddenly the pain and anguish that had locked her in seemed to melt away. She felt serenity and health flow back into her. The strange affliction was gone forever. Thérèse realized that she was cured.

4

Sacramental Moments

Thérèse's complete cure from her mysterious illness brought with it a deep peace. The Virgin's smile was real, although she did not know why the Mother of God would have personally intervened in her life. The answer for Thérèse, of course, was that Mary is and always remains a mother. She no longer had her own mother or Pauline who had taken her place. But Thérèse had Mary who would always remain a vital part of her life and spirituality.

Thérèse was puzzled because the nuns at Carmel were so intrigued by her smiling statue and the details of her cure. Perhaps she should not have let Marie tell them about the incident. Perhaps Thérèse could have been more clear in answering their questions. The memory of her illness became torture. She suffered a severe spiritual trial for four years. Because the nuns had their own ideas of the nature of her vision, Thérèse felt that she had lied both about her illness and the apparition of Our Lady. What was it? Had she done something to cause it? Was it from the devil? Whatever the factors involved, the Blessed Mother had smiled on her and cured her. She would continue to trust in the goodness of Mary and the mercy of Mary's Son.

During one visit to Carmel, Thérèse wondered out loud what name she would receive in religious life. "I knew there was a Sister Thérèse of Jesus; however, my beautiful name of Thérèse could not be taken away from me. All of a sudden I thought of *Little* Jesus whom I loved so much, and I said: 'Oh! How happy I would be if they would call me Thérèse of the Child Jesus!'" *(Story)* Mother Marie de Gonzague had thought of that name for Thérèse as well.

The Lord spoke to the child Thérèse in ordinary ways: through the good books she read and reread; through the holy pictures she had received from her teachers, especially one picture given her by Pauline. Thérèse describes it as "the *little flower* of the Divine Prisoner." She wrote: "Seeing that the name of Pauline was written under the little flower, I wanted Thérèse's name to be written there also and I offered myself to Jesus as his *little flower*" *(Story)*. The flower image would reappear throughout Thérèse's life. She saw herself as frail as a flower, but singularly strong because of Jesus' love for her. It was Jesus she knew who counts the birds, clothes the lilies and takes care of the grass of the fields.

Visit to Alençon

Thérèse was ten years old when Papa took his family back to Alençon for a two-week visit. This was Thérèse's first opportunity to return. Seeing the city once more opened the wound of her mother's death. She pictured the coffin and the tears of her family. Her ears rang with the sobs of her father and she felt again the loneliness.

This vacation cast a new image on Alençon. Thérèse witnessed the opposite ends of life's spectrum. The Martin's enjoyed their friends' villa, the parties, the festivities. The vacation passed quickly. Caught up in innocent fun, Thérèse would still pull back during quiet moments and compare the comfortable lifestyle of the family in Alençon with her goal to acquire eternal happiness hereafter. She was only ten but she realized that there were many more lessons to learn about life. Several years later, thinking back on the vacation in Alençon, Thérèse reminisced in her *Story of a Soul*. She had gone to pray at her mother's grave and had asked Mama to protect her always. She wrote about the lessons she had learned. About the family they stayed with in Alençon she observed: "The friends we had there were too worldly; they knew too well how to ally the joys of this earth to the service of God" *(Story)*.

Thérèse mused that their friends did not think enough about death, the sure reality. Although still a child, Thérèse had tasted death. It had struck her to the core of her existence. Death and life were intimately tied together. They were welded into one experience of life for every human being. It would have been easy to get caught up in the comfortable, the secure, but the *cross* dimension of the Gospel message was real. Thérèse would learn about the redemptive importance of suffering a little farther down the road on her spiritual journey.

First Communion Day

Three months before her First Communion, Pauline gave Thérèse a book she had made her to help her prepare for the special event. Thérèse fervently offered the little prayers and acts of virtue it suggested. Marie also gave her daily lessons. Thérèse felt that she had been thoroughly instructed and she waited anxiously for the day she would actually receive the Eucharistic Jesus. During Thérèse's lessons with Marie, the girl paid close attention as Marie emphasized that the Christian vocation is an invitation from the Lord to walk with him and to grow in holiness. What most impressed the child was Marie's conviction that sanctity was made up of small matters. Making choices to please God, to please Jesus, could consist of small sacrifices, ordinary actions like doing tasks diligently. Whatever a person did as part of his or her daily life, if performed to please Jesus, was an act of love for him.

This realization, that holiness does not depend on the greatness of our actions, but rather on the love and power of God acting in us, is the concept that would grow in young Thérèse. The Lord was to use her to remind the world once more that he is the God of love. This God of love is responsible for all the holiness that has ever been reflected in a human being since the beginning of time. Every saint, singled out by the Church as a model for imitation, owes his or her holiness to God. God is the initiator of all holiness and he it is who delights in his own reflection of goodness that a saint projects. A saint is a mirror of the image of God. Yet all the saints put together cannot equal the love of God. This is what Thérèse realized early in her life. Her journey in holiness would not be a triumph of heroic actions. It would not be a triumph in the eyes of those around her. The Lord was to let her spend twenty-four years on this earth living a lesson, being a lesson, not teaching with words, except through her writings. She would live out her existence singing a hymn made up of ordinary words that were magnificent to the ears of the God who is Love because Thérèse's song was rooted in Love.

Thérèse's desire to become a saint—to become close to God—surfaced during this time of preparation for her First Communion. It deepened because of Marie's thorough explanations and the clarity with which Marie could present her own spiritual wisdom. Thérèse realized in this experience that sanctity or holiness is ordinary. As she grew in the spiritual life, she would further emphasize the beauty of offering little acts of love to God—not for a reward but to please him. She grew in the awareness that God is the Divine Lover of each human soul. She realized that no one, not even Papa, or Pauline, or Marie, could ever love her as completely, as totally, as did God. This led her to abandon her life with trust to him. It sounds so easy, so uncomplicated, like the feat of an athlete who makes his performance look effortless. As Thérèse walked in confidence with Jesus, she began to see her own image reflected in his loving gaze.

Thérèse made a retreat at the boarding school. This was the immediate preparation for her First Communion. She treasured the spiritual conferences of Father Domin and copied down important points in her notebook. She appreciated the kindness of the nuns. During the retreat, Thérèse wore a large crucifix—a gift from Léonie—in her belt. This blessed object made her feel like a missionary.

The day finally arrived. The class, dressed in white, led into church, while voices sang the hymn: "O blessed altar ringed with angels." It was a day of true joy for Thérèse. She believed that the Eucharist is God, *her* God, and that he was coming into her soul in a very special and intimate way for the first time. She wept, blessed tears, not sad tears for the loss of her mother or regret that Pauline could not be there. Her tears were the result of being overwhelmed by the Divine Lover of her soul. She knew that the sacred host was God.

In the afternoon the first communicants made the Act of Consecration to Mary. Thérèse felt the closeness of Our Lady. In early evening, Papa and Thérèse walked to Carmel. Thérèse saw Pauline, her white veil crowned with roses, profess her vows as a Carmelite nun. Then Papa and his youngest daughter walked back home. Papa gave Thérèse a watch for her First Communion gift. And the day came to an end, a beautiful day that Thérèse would never forget.

The next day was joyful, too. But Thérèse mused that her beautiful gifts and pretty dress were still not enough to satisfy her. She wanted to receive Jesus again in holy communion. As frequent communion was not the custom in Thérèse's time, she was given permission by her parish priest to receive communion again on feast days. The next Church feast would be Ascension Day. As she knelt at the railing with Papa and Marie, she whispered in her heart the words of St. Paul, "I am alive not I but Christ lives in me" (cf. Galatians 2:20).

Confirmation

The evening before the feast days, Marie would sit down with Thérèse and share with her about the beauty of receiving the holy Eucharist. Thérèse listened attentively as her oldest sister spoke from her own experience about the power of Jesus in her life.

A short while after Thérèse's First Communion, she received another sacrament. Bishop Hugonin of Bayeux confirmed her on June 14, 1884. She wrote in her *Story of a Soul:* "I was prepared with great care to receive the visit of the Holy Spirit, and I did not understand why greater attention was not paid to the reception of this sacrament of *Love.*" The one day retreat of preparation at the abbey was extended to two when the bishop was delayed. Thérèse was delighted to have more time to pray and to prepare herself for the coming of divine Love.

This was such a special time because Confirmation was a marvelous link in Thérèse's spiritual life. As she had prepared to receive her second holy communion for Ascension Day, Marie had talked to her about something that burned into her soul. "I remember how once again she was speaking to me about suffering and she told me that I would probably not walk that way, that God would always carry me as a child. The day after my communion, the words of Marie came to my mind. I felt born within my heart a *great desire* to suffer, and at the same time the interior assurance that Jesus reserved a great number of crosses for me. I felt myself flooded with consolations so *great* that I look upon them as one of the *greatest* graces of my life" *(Story)*.

After Confirmation, Thérèse resumed her normal activities and found herself with students at school who were not serious enough about their faith or their studies. She felt uncomfortable with most of them. While she struggled to relate and to be accepted by her peers, she also wanted them to grow in maturity. "I had a happy disposition," she wrote, "but I didn't know how to enter into games of my age level. Often during the recreations, I leaned against a tree and studied my companions at a distance, giving myself up to serious reflections!" *(Story)*

But that was not all, soon Thérèse found a way to manifest her more serious approach to life. She and a few girlfriends began to bury the small dead birds gently gathered from around the property. The children surrounded the burials with appropriate ceremony. They planted small shrubs and flowers to enhance the beauty of the miniature cemetery.

Thérèse also tested her talents at storytelling. She invented a story and added to it daily during recreation time. Her audience grew and that increased her confidence. In fact, she noted in her *Story of a Soul* that even some of the older girls joined the listeners at times. But then the teacher put a stop to bird burying and storytelling. She wanted Thérèse and her friends to spend recreation time more actively.

Thérèse enjoyed learning and grasped her subjects. She excelled in catechism class. When Father Domin, the parish priest, orally quizzed the students, Thérèse answered the questions without missing a word. When, on rare occasions, she forgot an answer, tears would spill down her cheeks. The priest appreciated her efforts and gently encouraged her. He called Thérèse his *little doctor,* presuming her to be named after St. Teresa of Avila who was noted for her wisdom and holiness.

While Thérèse performed well in her classes, she notes in *Story of a Soul* that her relatives, the Guerins, thought of her as quiet and shy. She described her handwriting as a "terrible scrawl!" She did well at sewing and embroidery but did not know how to seek out admiration for what she had done. At this time in her life, she was underrated even by relatives. This helped Thérèse to learn to become indifferent to praise.

In friendships with children her own age, Thérèse manifested a loyalty and sensitiveness for others' likes and dislikes. She would give her friends little inexpensive gifts that she treasured but wanted to give up to please them. She poured out her love and care on her family, relatives and friends. Thérèse would one day channel her great love, making an offering of it to the One who was its Source, as she pronounced her vows at Carmel.

5

Growing Up

Marie joined Carmel in 1886, the same year that Thérèse became a member of the *Children of Mary*. Aunt Guerin invited Thérèse to stay a few weeks at the seashore. The family went in the summer to the seaside at Trouville. But without Céline, without Pauline, Marie, Léonie and, above all, Papa, the vacation was no fun. Thérèse soon became lonely and homesick. After a few days, she had to return to *Les Buissonnets*. Where would she find the courage a few years later to give her life to Jesus as a cloistered Carmelite religious? What power could transform this ordinary, homesick child into a person capable of giving her life totally to the Lord?

Because Thérèse records so many details of her years on earth in *Story of a Soul*, we can walk in the footsteps of her short life and watch her confront the struggles, hear her replies, share in her prayers, rejoice in her recognition of what God was doing for her.

Thérèse tells of some months when she was afflicted with scruples. She would worry about what she had said or done, fearing that she may have sinned. She was able to work through this with the help of Marie, who listened to her anxious disclosures and calmed her little sister. Marie encouraged Thérèse to deepen her love for Jesus who removes all fear. After Marie entered Carmel, Thérèse had no one to confide her fears of sin and weakness to. She prayed to her four deceased little brothers and sisters and confidently asked them to help and uplift her.

Chapter Five of *Story of a Soul* reveals a young woman coming out of childhood, yet reverting back from time to time. "I had a great desire, it is true, to practice virtue, but I went about it in a strange way," she observed. Until she entered the convent, she "didn't do any housework whatsoever." The family had hired help for domestic tasks. Thérèse recalls, however, that after Marie entered the convent, Céline took care of their bedroom. When Céline was away, Thérèse would make the bed and tidy the room. She noted that she did this for the love of God, but if Céline failed to realize or acknowledge Thérèse's act of love for God, Thérèse would be hurt and would shed tears. Acknowledging her extreme sensitiveness, Thérèse wrote: "God would have to work a little miracle to make me grow up in an instant."

Christmas Eve Miracle

On Christmas Eve, December 25, 1886, Thérèse received the grace of emerging from childhood. She was with the family at Midnight Mass. The Christ Child was just one hour old. In the crowded church, as the congregation sang Christmas carols and prepared to go back to their homes, Thérèse felt the power of Jesus touch her heart in a new way. He was offering her the opportunity to leave childhood behind forever. He was giving her the freedom to love him totally, to remain confident of his love, no matter what would happen. He was offering her peace of soul.

For the first time since she could remember, in an emotional moment, her eyes were dry. She had no tears. She felt peaceful and unafraid, convinced of the Lord's love for her.

The day had been long and busy. Papa felt tired as the family trudged home in the snow from Mass. Céline was excited because the family's youngest would still receive gifts in her shoes when they got home. Mr. Martin would have appreciated going straight to bed, but the shoes were by the fireplace. "Well, fortunately this will be the last year," Papa mumbled *(Story)*. Céline gasped softly. She knew Thérèse had heard the comment as she went upstairs to remove her hat and coat. Céline expected a flood of tears from her little sister. "Don't go downstairs," she said, fearing that Thérèse would find the situation too hard to take. But Thérèse understood her father's tiredness. There was nothing to be hurt about. No tears. She skipped quickly down the stairs and sat comfortably in front of the fireplace. One by one, she pulled the treasures from her shoes and proclaimed her joy. Papa caught the magic of the moment and forgot his fatigue. It was something Thérèse would never forget.

On this night, the *third phase* of her life began.

Awareness of the Sufferings of Christ

As a holy card of Jesus crucified slipped out of her missal one day, Thérèse's eyes fell on one of the Master's hands. It was pierced with a spike and blood was falling to the ground. The girl allowed her mind to penetrate the scene. She reflected that the blood of Jesus was being spilled for love of the people he came to redeem. But no one was there to catch that blood, to be cleansed by it. She felt the desire to be there for Jesus, at the foot of his cross, to make reparation—especially for sinners who had grown hard and bitter. She seemed to hear Jesus say to her: "I thirst." Thérèse realized that this was no physical thirst. It was deep in the soul of the Savior, who longed for sinners to let him touch their hearts, cure their spiritual ills, and bring them to himself. Thérèse told Jesus that she wanted to help quench his thirst. She wanted to offer her prayers and sacrifices for the souls of great sinners. Was this what Jesus was asking of her? Perhaps he would give her a favorable sign.

Pranzini, My Child

Thérèse learned of a man condemned to death for grave crimes. He would be dying within days. His name was Henri Pranzini. The newspaper carried accounts of his hardened attitude and the steel-like bitterness that closed in around him like a vice. Thérèse began to pray and offer sacrifices for her *child*, Pranzini. She talked Céline into going with her to the parish priest to arrange for the celebration of a Mass for Pranzini. The murderer's execution was set for August 31, 1887.

Thérèse had to know if her first spiritual child had shown some sign of repentance. She checked the newspaper the day after the execution for an account of what had happened. Paging through the *La Croix*, she quickly found what she was searching for. The condemned man had refused to go to confession before he had been taken to the scaffold. But a priest stood quietly by. He held a crucifix in his hands and watched anxiously for some sign that the man so near death would desire reconciliation with God. No sign came.

Then, the unexpected occurred. As Pranzini started to place his neck on the block, he looked up, turned his head toward the priest and asked for the crucifix. Father quickly held it out and the man kissed it reverently, three times. Then the guillotine's blade hit its mark and the repentant Pranzini was free.

Tears streamed down her cheeks as she shared her secret and the story of Pranzini's conversion with Céline. Pranzini would always be special to Thérèse. He was her first spiritual child. Jesus *was pleased* with her small sacrifices, with her prayers. This was the sign, such a glorious sign. There was nothing that Jesus could not accomplish through her. Thérèse had learned a valuable lesson even though she was just fourteen years old.

With her love for Jesus growing and her desire to save sinners for the love of Jesus, Thérèse was freed from two of her own spiritual problems. Her scruples disappeared and her extreme sensitivity was overcome. She had helped Jesus to free Pranzini, and now she too was really free.

6

The Magnet

Evidence of the Christmas miracle surfaced daily in Thérèse's young life. She longed to be a channel of Jesus' love for the people of her time. Thérèse wanted to save souls. She desired to lead people to Jesus. She had developed a *spiritual thirst* to make Jesus known and loved. While she wanted others to love the Lord, her own love increased as well. "I slaked his thirst and the more I gave him *to drink,* the more the thirst of my poor little soul increased, and it was this ardent thirst he was giving me as the most delightful drink of his love" *(Story).*

Serene days lay ahead. Thérèse felt a deep interior joy. No longer tied down by anxiety and scrupulosity, her mind was free. She had always loved learning. Now she wanted to study useful subjects beyond what she was learning from her tutor, Madame Papinau. "I applied myself to some special studies in *history* and *science* and I did this on my own" *(Story).* Thérèse pondered her study habits and weighed her motives for studying in the light of Scripture and the spiritual classic with which she was most familiar: *The Imitation of Christ.* In Ecclesiastes 2:11, Thérèse read: "Then I considered all that my hands had done and the toil I had spent in doing it, and again, all was vanity and a chasing after wind, and there was nothing to be gained under the sun."

Thérèse also kept in mind chapter three of *The Imitation of Christ* which speaks of the right use of knowledge. She confined her reading to certain times and hours to "mortify my intense desire to know things" *(Story)*. One part of her was pulled toward the good things of this life. Another part of her reached far beyond her years to weigh circumstances in the light of eternity. She speaks of being nourished on the pure flour of *The Imitation of Christ* and the honey and oil of Father Arminjon's book "on the end of the present world and the mysteries of the future life" *(Story)*.

Papa had Father Arminjon's book on loan from the Carmelite nuns and Thérèse asked to read it. She sat near the window of her study and rested the book on the sill. Slowly she read and reread the book that spoke to her of the mysteries of faith and eternal life. Thérèse was consoled by her belief in an afterlife. She was young, but already could claim a big investment in that hope. Her mother, as well as her two brothers and two of her sisters were alive in God. Paul wrote: "If for this life only we have hoped in Christ, we are of all people most to be pitied" (1 Cor 15:19). Thérèse weighed the greatness of eternal life with the sacrifices that daily living would require of her. She came to the conclusion that no matter what those sacrifices might be, they were worth it if enduring them with love could lead to eternity with God.

Father Arminjon's reflections on the perfect love of God intrigued Thérèse. She felt as though her heart was drawn by a magnet to the heart of the Savior. "I wanted to *love, to love Jesus with a passion,* giving him a thousand proofs of my love while it was possible" *(Story)*. She prayed to Jesus, letting the love he placed in her heart be her guide.

Céline and Thérèse—Spiritual Sisters

When Thérèse was small, the three and a half years between her and her nearest sister, Céline, seemed great. Thérèse wanted very much to be a part of Céline's world, but Céline remained silent and aloof. She told her little sister that she would have to grow "'as high as a stool' so that she could have confidence in me" *(Story)*. Thérèse would climb up on the stool and beg Céline to let her in on her grown-up world, but still Céline refused. Then suddenly Céline's whole attitude toward Thérèse changed. Céline became trusting and open. She treated her youngest sister as an equal. The distance which had separated them disappeared.

Thérèse wrote: "Jesus, wanting to have us advance together, formed bonds in our hearts stronger than blood. He made us become *spiritual sisters*" *(Story)*. Thérèse reflected in *Story of a Soul* that the friendship she and Céline experienced was the type spoken of by St. John of the Cross in his *Spiritual Canticle.* The spiritual conversations the two sisters shared brought hours of delight to both of them. Thérèse likened those precious times to the conversations St. Monica had with her converted son, Augustine. As the two saints spoke of their longing for heaven and the presence of God, it seemed as if they could experience some of the joy their faith told them they would find at the journey's end. Thérèse and Céline, in their young hearts, felt something of the same.

The spiritual life grew in its attraction. Thérèse felt the desire to make little sacrifices and renunciations for the love of Jesus. Motivation was important to her. She wanted to do things not for a heavenly reward, but to please Jesus. At first, the renunciations cost her dearly. Sometimes, she admits, her face betrayed the struggle. But as time passed, with the help of prayer, and encouraged by Céline's efforts, Thérèse found joy in self-sacrifice.

At this time too, she would have loved to receive holy communion daily, a privilege rarely given before the pontificate of Pope St. Pius X (1903–1914). Thérèse received communion as often as her confessor permitted but believed in frequent holy communion. She prayed that the Church would not only permit daily communion but foster it. That day would come not too many years after her death. Thérèse's confessor invited her to receive the Eucharist four times a week during the month of May and added a fifth when a feast occurred. When the priest gave her this permission, the girl left the confessional with tears of gratitude streaming down her cheeks and a radiant smile. All she could think of was the joy of receiving Jesus.

The Inner Call

Everything that happened in Thérèse's life was part of a plan, unfolding piece by piece, like a giant puzzle. These pieces fell together and revealed the road that was opening to her. She felt within her soul an invitation, a call spoken by the Master. She had become attuned to Jesus, who was leading her so carefully to himself. How would she share his life in his Church? It seemed so clear to her even though she was just fourteen years old: Thérèse would be a Carmelite nun. Like Pauline and Marie before her, she, too, felt drawn to Carmel.

Thérèse wanted to share her secret with Céline but was sensitive to the fact that Céline may have been discerning a religious vocation. When Thérèse manifested her own desire, Céline realized that if Thérèse entered Carmel, the two great friends would be separated. She also realized that everything would work out no matter which of the girls entered first. Céline encouraged Thérèse in every way. There is not even a hint in *Story of a Soul* that Céline showed any resentment that Thérèse was trying to plunge ahead. At Carmel, Marie bluntly told Thérèse that she was too young, but Pauline encouraged her.

Thérèse chose the feast of Pentecost to ask Papa's permission. It was May 29, 1887. She had turned fourteen in January. Mr. Martin sat at the edge of the well in the backyard garden. Thérèse found him and sat next to him. Her eyes glistened with unshed tears.

Gentle Papa put his arm around his youngest child. "What's the matter my *little queen?*" he asked. They rose and walked slowly down the path back and forth, Thérèse's head on Papa's strong chest. She told him of her desire to become a Carmelite and she asked his permission to enter the convent as soon as possible. Papa's tears mingled with his daughter's, but he didn't try to discourage her. He noted that she was very young, yet he knew the Lord would take care of her.

Mr. Martin went over to the garden wall and gently uprooted a small white flower from a crevice. He handed it to his *little queen,* and explained that it was Jesus' love and care that had nurtured the flower until that very moment. Thérèse realized by analogy that she was like that little flower, cherished by Jesus and his heavenly Father. Thérèse took the flower and pressed it in her copy of *The Imitation of Christ.* She believed that the delicate flower would soon be transplanted to Carmel.

7

Beyond the Miracle

Uncle Guerin, Mr. Martin's trusted advisor in family matters, was the next person Thérèse confided her desire to. She approached him with the confidence that his reaction would duplicate Papa's. Unfortunately, her uncle was not in the same frame of mind. On October 8, 1887, Thérèse had a talk with him. "He forbade me to speak about my vocation to him until I was seventeen," she wrote in *Story of a Soul.* "It was contrary to human prudence, he said, to have a child of fifteen enter Carmel." To impress his young niece with the seriousness of his decision, Uncle Guerin shouted that it would take a miracle for him to give his consent. Thérèse realized that prolonging her conversation with her uncle was useless. She slipped quietly out of the room and took her problem to Jesus in prayer. Papa had been the perfect person to start with. It was Papa who backed her, was there for her, made time for her and showered her with the love of a father and a mother. Perhaps Papa could persuade Uncle Guerin. But in her heart Thérèse knew that the only one who turns hearts around is God. She continued her prayers, asking Jesus with all her youthful confidence for a miracle.

Two weeks passed by, which Thérèse referred to in *Story of a Soul* as "a long time." Thérèse reflected on Scripture imagery that matched her mood and offered consolation. She pondered the anxiety of Mary and Joseph who searched three days for Jesus before finding him in the temple. From Wednesday, October 19, until Saturday, October 22, Thérèse felt unusually sad. Everything around her seemed to fade into night. She could not sense the nearness of Jesus. It was as if he were hiding from her. The skyline of her soul was dark, without even a streak of light on the horizon. The weather matched her mood. Everything was gray. On Saturday, she went to the Guerins to visit, half hoping to talk to her uncle again about her vocation and half fearing to try.

Uncle Guerin greeted Thérèse as she visited with her cousins. Then he called her into his study. He began speaking, gently, unlike their previous encounter. First he chided her for being afraid of him. Then he humbly told her that she would not have to beg for a miracle to change his decision about her vocation…"the miracle had been granted…. Without making any allusion whatsoever to 'human prudence,' he told me I was a little flower God wanted to gather, and he would no longer oppose it!" (Story) The next day, Sunday, October 23, Thérèse paid a visit to Carmel to tell her sisters the wonderful news. She had her heart set on entering Carmel on the Christmas following her conversion. Pauline, in her quiet way, broke the news that the superior of Carmel said that she could not enter the Order until she was twenty-one.

The Carmelite nuns explained that Thérèse would have to be interviewed by the priest superior of the Carmelite community in Lisieux. On the agreed upon date, she and Papa were greeted by a straight-faced, soft spoken priest who ushered them into his office. Papa looked reassuringly at his daughter and Thérèse glanced from her father to the priest, searching anxiously for just a trace of a welcome on the cleric's face. He was serious and succinct. Thérèse said that he "received us coldly" *(Story)*. The guests would hardly have had to sit down.

Thérèse was much too young, she was told bluntly. Her father immediately spoke up in her defense. But the superior had made up his mind. He added, though, that if the bishop thought otherwise, there would be no more objection from him. The interview was over. The girl and her father had been treated as if they were interruptions in a very important schedule. There was nothing to do but leave and they did, quietly, the old man's arm around his daughter's shoulder. Tears streamed down Thérèse's face. They went outside and quickly put up their umbrellas for protection against the pouring rain.

Papa reassured Thérèse and encouraged her on the walk home. He groped for words to console her. How many young people have a totally selfish outlook on life, he must have thought. All his *little queen* wanted was to follow her religious vocation. As they walked, Thérèse mentioned that she wanted to go to see the bishop in Bayeux. Her father promised to accompany her and support her. Louis Martin became as determined as his daughter. He promised to take her to the Holy Father, Pope Leo XIII, if it would prove necessary.

The Meeting with Bishop Hugonin

Mr. Martin and Thérèse journeyed to Bayeux to keep their appointment with the bishop. It was October 31, 1887. As they approached the episcopal residence, which looked to Thérèse like a palace, she felt her old shyness enveloping her. If only Papa would do the talking, but he had asked Thérèse to present her own request and explanation. She wished one or more of her sisters could be with her.

In Bayeux, the rain poured down in steady torrents.

Mr. Martin did not want his daughter to appear rain-soaked before the bishop, so they took a bus to the cathedral to wait until the rain had stopped. A large group of worshipers were attending a funeral as the Martins slipped into the first pew. Thérèse realized that in her bright dress and white hat she was a contrast to the black-clad mourners in the pews. After the funeral, she and Papa waited in the small chapel behind the main altar for the rain to stop. When they could finally leave, Papa looked quickly around the cathedral's interior at the inspiring sight. But Thérèse could not focus on the church. She was on a mission to see the bishop. One part of her was overjoyed for the opportunity to plead her case. Another part of her dreaded the encounter.

The appointment had been made through the bishop's secretary, Father Reverony. The Martins went to his office. Even though the priest had expected them, he was not able to be there. Patiently, Mr. Martin took his daughter and toured the city on a bus. They had lunch and rested in a lovely hotel near the bishop's residence. When they returned a second time to Father Reverony's office, he was in. He brought father and daughter into his study and listened to Thérèse's explanation of her reason for wanting to see the bishop. She was now almost there. Still Father Reverony had to make the visit happen. According to Thérèse's account in *Story of a Soul*, Father Reverony was kind and welcoming. He seemed surprised about the purpose of her wanting to see the bishop. But after asking a few simple questions, he said, "I am going to introduce you to the bishop; will you kindly follow me?"

Tears rushed to Thérèse's eyes. Perhaps they were tears of relief. She would finally fufilll the purpose of this visit. Father Reverony suggested that she hide her tears from the bishop. They walked through several ornate rooms with large, comfortable-looking chairs. Portraits of bishops adorned the walls; Thérèse felt smaller and smaller as she and Papa advanced toward the bishop's study.

Bishop Hugonin was the prelate of Bayeux and Lisieux from 1867 until his death in 1898. He entered the room and the Martins kissed his ring. Thérèse sat in the big chair selected for her by Father Reverony. How she wished Papa would explain the purpose of their visit, but she knew that this was her moment to speak. She gave her reasons for wanting to enter Carmel at her young age rather than having to wait until she was twenty-one. She was convinced and certain in her heart, but her own words sounded wooden and unimpassioned. She finished and looked anxiously at the prelate. The bishop asked Thérèse if she had wanted to enter the Carmelite convent for a long time.

"Oh, yes," Thérèse came back, "for a very long time."

"It couldn't have been fifteen years," Father Reverony smilingly interjected.

Thérèse blushed. "That's true," she responded, "but there aren't too many years to subtract because I wanted to be a religious since the dawn of my reason, and I wanted Carmel as soon as I knew about it. I find all the aspirations of my soul are fulfilled in this Order" *(Story)*.

The bishop gently suggested how consoling it would be for her father if Thérèse would remain at home for a few more years. But Mr. Martin quickly came to his daughter's support and assured the bishop of his readiness to let his daughter enter then, at the age of fifteen. The bishop said that he would have to speak with the superior of Carmel in Lisieux. Thérèse felt beaten and drained. After all she and Papa had been through on the journey to Carmel, was it to end back in the hands of Father Delatroette? Aware of the priest's adamant refusal, Thérèse's tears spilled over and slid uncontrollably down her cheeks. The bishop was moved. He put his arm around Thérèse's neck and bent her head onto his shoulder. He told her to have courage, to go on her pilgrimage to Rome and to rejoice because the trip to the Eternal City would strengthen her in her vocation.

The informal procession moved into the garden as they walked toward the gate. Mr. Martin couldn't resist telling Bishop Hugonin that Thérèse had worn her hair piled neatly on top of her head in an attempt to appear older. The bishop was to tell that story many times later on when speaking of Thérèse.

Mr. Martin then asked about a few details concerning the coming pilgrimage. Father Reverony would be guiding the pilgrimage, and Papa wanted specifics about what he and his two young daughters, Céline and Thérèse, should wear for the papal audience. The priest answered the questions then accompanied Mr. Martin and Thérèse to the gate and shut it gently behind them.

Outside the floodgates broke open and Thérèse sobbed on Papa's shoulder. She was disappointed for herself, true, but also for Papa who had planned to send a telegram to the Carmel of Lisieux announcing that the bishop had granted his permission for Thérèse to enter Carmel at fifteen. Years later she wrote of this sad event: "My soul was plunged into bitterness but into peace too, for I was seeking God's will" *(Story)*.

8

The Pilgrimage

Louis Martin and his two youngest daughters, eighteen-year-old Céline and fifteen-year-old Thérèse blended in with excited pilgrims at the Lisieux train station. They were to be there at 3:00 A.M. on that crisp November 4th. The Martins were on time and fully awake. This pilgrimage was special, combining the pilgrims of two dioceses: Bayeux and the neighboring diocese, Coutances. The event was to honor Pope Leo XIII's fifty years of priesthood.

Pope Leo XIII had been elected to the See of St. Peter in 1878. His twenty-five year reign would span the new century and last until his death in 1903. The people who signed up for the pilgrimage felt a mixture of excitement and awe. They were going to travel to several famous cities as tourists, but more than that, they would be on a spiritual journey. The Martins felt that same excitement, but for Thérèse, the journey had particular signicance. Before she would return home to Lisieux she would have met the Pope and have spoken to him. Her heart beat faster at the thought of it. She had pictured the audience in her imagination. She had seen portraits of Pope Leo XIII and could imagine him smiling at her and speaking with her. She could even hear his voice, a soft, calm voice like Papa's.

The pilgrimage would conclude in this same train station nearly a month later. What adventures and excitement would fill that month.

The itinerary of the French pilgrims would include stops in Paris, France, Switzerland, and various cities of Italy: Milan, Venice, Bologna, Loreto, Rome, Naples, Pompeii, Assisi, Florence, Pisa and Genoa. They were to make a return visit to Pisa and Genoa before arriving back in Lisieux on December 2, 1887.

The train pulled into the Paris station in the morning. Mr. Martin was anxious to show his girls the magnificent sites. They spent the next few days on their own, then joined up with the pilgrimage group on November 7. Thérèse enjoyed Paris, but what most impressed her was Our Lady of Victories shrine. Before the statue of the Blessed Virgin, Thérèse prayed earnestly to her heavenly mother. Her thoughts carried her back into the pages of her early life, when Mary had been especially near her. After Thérèse's mother had left this earth, Jesus' mother had cared for her. Thérèse felt the same gratitude toward Mary that she had experienced on her First Communion day, five years earlier. Thérèse called her "Mama" and asked to be hidden "beneath the shadow of her virginal mantle!" *(Story)* She asked *Mama* to "keep far from me everything that could tarnish my purity." The Martins also visited the Basilica at Montmarte and consecrated themselves to the Sacred Heart of Jesus. Then they were ready for their journey.

On November 7, the pilgrims left Paris. They were directed to their seats on the train. Each of the cars was named after a saint. The Martins were assigned to the St. Martin car, much to the delight of their father. The train started chugging down the track, slowly at first, then gathering speed. "Papa was very happy," Thérèse records in

Story of a Soul, "when the train began to move he sang the old refrain, '*Roll, roll, my carriage, here we are on the open road.*'" The Martins made friends with the other pilgrims. They enjoyed the people and the people enjoyed them. Thérèse was delighted to feel at home and unafraid. "I was talking freely with the great ladies, the priests, and even the bishop of Coutances" *(Story)*. This bishop led the pilgrimage. Thérèse recalled that when she would slip away into the group, her father, her *king*, would gently call her back and invite her to loop her arm through his, the way she did when they went on their walks in Lisieux. Bishop Hugonin's secretary, Father Reverony, was also a pilgrim. Thérèse noted in her autobiography that the priest kept an eye on her and Céline. Frequently the priest would lean forward at the dinner table to watch Thérèse or to better hear her conversation. No doubt he found interesting a young person so normal yet so firm in her conviction of her religious vocation. By the end of the pilgrimage Father Reverony seemed convinced of Thérèse's call, but at the papal audience in Rome he would prove himself to be a stumbling block.

The train crept like a caterpillar through the mountains and valleys of Switzerland. Thérèse watched small villages with little cottages glide by. White clouds floated along. As the sun set across a large lake, the water shimmered in the reflection. This panorama of nature's beauty etched itself deeply into Thérèse's memory.

Stepping Stones to Rome

Milan was their first Italian stop on the way to Rome. The pilgrims gazed at the magnificent white marble cathedral. They climbed the steps and entered to view the interior. Statues of saints "formed a small population" *(Story)*. Huge pillars held up the structure and dwarfed the travel-

ers. The Martins stayed close to the bishop to hear his
explanation of the saints' relics. They participated in his
Mass at the tomb of St. Charles Borromeo, once the
bishop of Milan. Those who were physically able climbed
to the top of the bell tower and stepped onto the roof.
They scanned the city below. People walking along the
streets seemed as tiny as insects. After the cathedral the
pilgrims were taken on the first of a series of tours. They
stopped at a unique cemetery called *Campo Santo*. The
marble statues which marked the graves were lifelike carv-
ings of individuals performing tasks that belong to the
living. Thérèse noticed a statue of a child scattering flowers on the grave of its parents. The petals were so life-like
that they seemed to float in the breeze. Belief in heaven, in
an afterlife, was evident in the city's churches and monuments that spoke eloquently of the faith of the people who
revered them.

The pilgrims went on to Venice, city of waterways and
gondoliers. Then to Padua where the Martins venerated
the tongue of St. Anthony of Padua. Next came Bologna
where they prayed before the remains of St. Catherine of
Bologna. The pilgrims arrived there at a busy time. Students, some too carefree, were crowding the train stations
and streets. One of the young men latched on to Thérèse
and tried to drag her away. "But I gave him such a look he
soon let go!" *(Story)* Meanwhile, Céline was coming to the
assistance of her youngest sister. In the confusion of the
crowded station, Papa was struggling to find all the lug-
gage and did not notice Thérèse's predicament. Thérèse
was anxious to depart for the next stop on the journey:
Loreto. There the Martins toured the *Holy House* which
has long been venerated as the home of the Holy Family
miraculously transported to Loreto from Nazareth.
Thérèse and Céline left Papa with the tourists to partici-

pate at Mass at the main altar of the basilica. The two sisters found a priest who by special privilege was celebrating Mass in the *Holy House* itself. Thérèse and Céline asked Father if they could receive communion at his Mass. He immediately asked for two small hosts. The Martin girls knelt devoutly as Father began the Eucharist. Then at communion time, they received their Lord. Thérèse remembered the event so vividly as she wrote in her *Story of a Soul* nearly ten years later that it seemed it had happened just a few days before.

The pilgrimage continued on schedule. The next part of the journey would bring them to Rome.

Rome at Last

The pilgrim train pulled into Rome's train station late at night. The passengers woke to the porters' shouts announcing their arrival in the city of popes and martyrs. The Martins looked forward to spending eight days in the eternal city. Thérèse clung to the most exciting dream of all: her visit with Pope Leo XIII which would take place on the seventh day. The first day the Martins and the other pilgrims toured the outskirts, taking in the impressive Roman monuments. Thérèse noticed the peacefulness of the countryside, uncluttered by commercial influence. Parts of the city of Rome, on the other hand, were marked by something of a secular atmosphere, reminding her of Paris.

During the coming days, Thérèse and Céline were dazzled by the sights, especially by the Coliseum. While Papa stood attentively listening to the tour guide, his girls slipped under the construction barricade and descended into the arena. They searched for and found the stone with a cross etched into it, hallowing the spot where many martyrs had given their lives for Jesus.

Thérèse writes in her *Story of a Soul,* "My heart was beating hard when my lips touched the dust stained with the blood of the first Christians. I asked for the grace of being a martyr for Jesus and felt that my prayer was answered!" *(Story)* As the two girls rejoined the group of pilgrims, Papa nodded and smiled. How could he be upset at the fervor of his impetuous daughters?

The pilgrims toured the catacombs and Thérèse took some earth from the tomb of St. Cecilia as a relic of the martyred saint. Thérèse was thrilled to actually stand in Cecilia's tomb. She also visited the saint's home, the site of her martyrdom. The pilgrims learned that Cecilia had been proclaimed *patroness of music* by the Church. This was not because she played an instrument or sang beautifully, but because she had sung a song to Jesus, the Spouse of her heart, when she was being martyred.

Thérèse and Céline were impressed by this heroine. They were attracted by her virginal love for the Lord. They too wanted to sing a song to their Spouse, to give him their hearts. "I felt more than devotion for her; it was the real tenderness of a friend" *(Story)*. The Martins then visited the Church of St. Agnes, Agnes being Pauline's religious name in Carmel. Meanwhile, the days passed and Thérèse's excitement and anxiety mounted as Sunday's papal audience drew near.

Sunday, November 20, 1887, would always be remembered by Thérèse, who just ten short years later would find herself in eternity. Yet in the decade that remained to her, the Lord would accomplish great things in Thérèse's soul. In a sense, Thérèse's vocation would begin at the feet of Pope Leo XIII and linger at the nailed feet of the Crucified. But that would not be the whole of the journey, although Thérèse's life was marked with the cross. Her story would end in victory, sealed in the glory of Jesus.

The Papal Audience

The pilgrims gathered in the papal chapel for Mass at 8:00 A.M. Pope Leo moved reverently through the Mass. He was prayerful and intent. Thérèse could hardly take her eyes off him. Her thoughts raced ahead to the audience which was to follow. Her pulse beat more quickly and her cheeks burned. At communion time, she poured out her anticipation to Jesus, really present within her. He understood; she knew he did and very soon, in minutes, she would be able to voice her simple request to the pope. She glanced over at Céline whose eyes met hers in a quick knowing look. Everything seemed to be a sign from God of his special interest and concern. The Gospel of the Sunday liturgy was proclaimed: "Do not be afraid, little flock, for it is your Father's good pleasure to give you the kingdom" (Lk 12:32).

After Mass, the pilgrims formed a line and knelt one by one before Pope Leo XIII, kissing his slipper and his ring. The pope in turn blessed each one. Thérèse's turn came. Moments before, Father Reverony, in a solemn tone, had announced that none of the pilgrims was to speak privately to the pope because time was at a minimum. Thérèse had felt panic racing through her. She turned to Céline who was behind her. "What should I do?" she whispered. "Speak," Céline said decisively.

Thérèse stepped forward and knelt before the pope. She kissed the Holy Father's slipper and ring. Blotting out the stern face of Father Reverony, mounted at the pope's side, she leaned forward. Her innocent gray eyes pierced the heart of Pope Leo who instinctively leaned forward to listen. She gazed up at him and blurted out in one sentence the only request she had of the Church: "'Holy Father, in honor of your jubilee, permit me to enter Carmel at the age of fifteen!'" *(Story)* What passed through

the pope's mind when he looked at this young woman?
How different were their paths in life. Leo XIII would be
one of the longest-reigning popes in history: from 1878
until 1903—twenty-five years. Thérèse would live just
twenty-four years and nine months. She knelt before him
just as she was: a person in a hurry. She seemed to sense
that she didn't have much time.

Father Reverony told the Holy Father that Thérèse was
a *child* who wanted to enter Carmel at the age of fifteen.
He could have reinforced her request, but he did not.
Resting her folded hands on the pope's knees, Thérèse
made a final impassioned plea. "Oh! Holy Father, if you
say yes, everybody else will agree!" *(Story)* The pope gazed
intently down at her. "Go...go.... *You will enter if God wills
it!*" he responded *(Story)*. Thérèse tried to speak again, but
Pope Leo placed his index finger over her lips. Two
guards appeared out of nowhere. Gently, efficiently, they
took an elbow each and lifted Thérèse across the room
and into the waiting area. Tears blinded her eyes.

The audience of Papa and the other men followed the
women. Papa was introduced by Father Reverony as the
father of two Carmelite nuns. Pope Leo was impressed and
placed his hand affectionately on Louis Martin's head.
Thérèse's father glowed as he thought of Marie and
Pauline, his two oldest children, united with them in
spirit. Oh, if Zelie could only be here to share in the joy of
this moment. Yet something told him that she *was* there.
She *did* know. Two regal papal guards assisted Mr. Martin
as they had each pilgrim, guiding them to the adjoining
waiting room. After the audience, Thérèse calmed down
and made an act of trust in Jesus. Whatever God wanted,
she wanted, and she knew he would give her the grace to
believe in that prayer. Jesus was silent as Thérèse and her
family left the Vatican. The tears continued to stream

down her cheeks, but Thérèse was at peace. She stepped with her father and Céline out into the pouring rain.

The Pilgrimage Concludes

What did Jesus want of Thérèse? At this point in her young life, she could give him her total trust. She prayed an act of confidence and felt renewed strength. There was a reason for everything, she knew that. And even though she could not see beyond the roadblocks that seemed to prevent her from following her dream, she believed everything would work out. To doubt that would be to doubt Jesus himself, and that was unthinkable. She remembered the account of Jesus being asleep in the boat and the apostles' fear of drowning in the storm. The Lord was asleep in Thérèse's boat too. But she trusted that he would awake and take matters into his sure hands.

The pilgrims traveled on to Naples, Pompeii and Assisi. It was in Assisi that Thérèse lost the buckle on her dress. While she searched for it, the carriages pulled away. She was left behind with the last carriage of the pilgrimage. Thérèse looked up at the passengers and her face turned crimson. The carriage belonged to Father Reverony, the very last person in the world that Thérèse wanted to ride with. All the passenger seats were taken, but one gentleman quickly jumped out and joined the driver and Father Reverony invited Thérèse to enter.

As the carriage bounced along, the priest went out of his way to be gracious and pleasant. He no longer wore the stern look that he had maintained during the papal audience. His voice was kind and respectful. He chatted with Thérèse on an adult level. When the carriage arrived at the station, the wealthy passengers pulled out their large purses and opened them to tip the carriage driver. Thérèse looked around at the important people and felt she should do the same. She opened her purse and found some coins. Father Reverony gently told her not to think of it. He paid for both Thérèse and himself. Perhaps the priest thought of the example of Jesus who had helped Peter to provide payment of the temple tax for them both.

The pilgrims stopped in Florence, then passed once more through Pisa and Genoa on their way home to France. They arrived back in Lisieux on the afternoon of December 2, 1887.

9

Gaze Set on Carmel

After her return, Thérèse went to visit the nuns at Carmel. So much had happened since her last visit. Papa had just offered her the opportunity to go on another pilgrimage, this time to Jerusalem. But Thérèse quickly declined. While the thought of the Holy Land was appealing, the invitation had come too soon. She had just experienced one train ride too many; one coach ride too many. She wanted nothing other than to walk firmly on solid ground and to enjoy Lisieux's familiar streets.

She visited Carmel and was particularly grateful for the time she could pour out thoughts and adventures—a whole month's worth—to Pauline. Now what more could Thérèse do to obtain permission to enter Carmel? Pauline suggested that Thérèse write to Bishop Hugonin to remind him of his promise to contact her about the matter. Thérèse went home and did as Pauline suggested. Uncle Guerin felt that her letter was too simple. He helped her to draft another. Just when they were going to mail it, Thérèse received a message from Pauline to hold on to it for a few days. On December 15, the letter was finally mailed. Thérèse longed for the bishop's instant reply. She wanted to spend this Christmas at home in Carmel. Every morning after Mass Papa patiently accompanied her to the post office. Each day brought another disappointment—

no letter from the bishop. Christmas drew nearer. Papa's heart ached for his youngest child. Perhaps his heart ached a little for himself, too. What would the first Christmas without his *little queen* be like? But Christmas this year would come and go as it always had, with his *little queen* by his side. Jesus wanted Thérèse to be home at *Les Buissonnets,* that is where he would find her. Thérèse thought of it as if the Child Jesus had fallen asleep. His toys were left untended in a corner. He still loved the toys, but because he was a real human as well as a divine child, he had the needs of a child. And so he slept. He took his nap while Thérèse waited for him to wake.

After Midnight Mass, the Martins returned home to continue their celebration of the Savior's birth. When Céline and Thérèse made their way to their room, Thérèse was greeted with a delightful surprise. Artistic Céline had decorated a washbasin to give the appearance of a little pond. She had crafted a sailboat and placed it in the center. The boat contained an image of the Child Jesus holding a ball in his hand. The sail of the boat had a hand-painted message from Scripture: "I sleep, but my heart watches" (Canticle of Canticles 5:2). On the side of the boat was the word *abandonment.*

Glimpse of a Carmelite Christmas

On Christmas afternoon, the Martins paid a short visit to Carmel. When the curtain covering the grille opened, Thérèse's eyes fixed on the infant Jesus. He held a ball in his hand, symbolic of Thérèse's expression that she was a toy of Jesus that could be lavished with attention or forgotten. The ball had Thérèse's name on it. Then the nuns sang a hymn for her that had been composed by Pauline. Thérèse was overwhelmed by their thoughtfulness. She exclaimed her gratitude through a steady stream of tears.

The Final Delay

On January 1, 1888, a letter was delivered to Thérèse. It was from Mother Marie de Gonzague who informed Thérèse that the bishop's permission for her immediate entrance to Carmel had arrived at Carmel on December 28, 1887. Mother de Gonzague explained that she had decided to delay telling Thérèse until January 1. But there was more. Mother had also decided that Thérèse should not enter until after Lent, which would mean a delay of three more months. Although Thérèse could not assume the reasons or dare to ask, it would seem logical that the prioress wished to spare the young applicant the rigors of a Carmelite Lent.

Time passed. Thérèse particularly treasured the days she still had with Céline. The girls shared spiritual conversations and good times together. Thérèse wanted to spend her remaining months preparing to enter Carmel. In *Story of a Soul* she presented her approach to self-denial and mortification. She explained that she never performed heroic penances of which great saints were capable. Thérèse wrote simply that she was never attracted to severe mortifications. Instead she revealed: "My mortifications consisted in breaking my will, always so ready to impose itself on others, in holding back a reply, in rendering little services without any recognition, in not leaning my back against a support when seated, etc., etc. It was through the practice of these *nothings* that I prepared myself to become the fiancée of Jesus, and I cannot express how much this waiting left me with sweet memories."

The Long Road Home

The distance from *Les Buissonnets* to Carmel was short even on foot. But what a long journey it had been for fifteen-year-old Thérèse. The night before she entered the convent, her family and close relatives shared a meal and evening together. Thérèse was touched by the love and affection each showed her. Their confidence in the maturity of her decision meant so much to her. Papa was quiet, but gazed at Thérèse often. Where had the years gone? If only Zelie could be there now for this wonderful moment. He couldn't help but realize the loneliness he would bear after the departure of his youngest daughter. Yet her happiness made it worth the personal loss. That was Papa's approach to all his children. But life was going to be much more ordinary without Thérèse. No more frantic walks to the post office. No more tear sessions or visits to Bishop Hugonin. No more pilgrimages or afternoon walks or picnics or Eucharistic visits with the *little queen*. Mr. Martin's memory was filled with a panorama of events that he would always treasure.

The next morning Thérèse linked her arm in Papa's just as she had done so often in years gone by. Her family and relatives met for Mass at the monastery chapel and received communion together. As they prayed in thanksgiving, they wept. It was a wonderful day and yet a sad day too. Good-byes are always hard. And even though Thérèse would live near them in the same town, the cloistered life she was choosing would restrict them from seeing her. It was true that when Thérèse left *Les Buissonnets* on April 9, 1888, she was never to see her home again.

From the chapel, Thérèse and Papa went to the enclosure door. There, Thérèse knelt and asked her father's blessing. Papa carefully traced the sign of the cross on her forehead. Then he helped her up. While they hugged, they wept. This was the hardest part of all: to leave Papa, *her* king, in order to find the *King of kings*.

PART 2

"I come before you with empty hands.
All the secret store of grace I fling into needy hearts,
crying in the bitter night of fear and loneliness.
Spendthrift of your Love, I keep before me
your empty hands—
empty and riven with the great nails
hollowing out rivers of mercy,
until all your substance was poured out.

"So I, my Jesus, with hands emptied for your love,
stand confident before your cross,
love's crimson emblem.
It is the empty who are filled:
those who have made themselves
spendthrifts, for you alone fill the least of your brethren
while they themselves are nourished by your love . . .
more and more emptied that
they may be filled with you."

Thérèse as a novice, 1889.

Thérèse with her novices, Mother Marie de Gonzague and Mother Agnes.

10

The Carmel of Lisieux

The doors of Carmel closed and Mother Marie de Gonzague came forward to embrace Thérèse. Then Pauline and Marie hugged her. Thérèse could hardly believe she had finally arrived. She looked around the softly lit hallway and wondered what the rest of the monastery was like. She was just beginning her religious life as a *postulant*. Thérèse was led to the nun's chapel, called the choir. The Blessed Sacrament was exposed. The choir was dim so that the worshippers on the other side of the grille could adore the Eucharist but would be unable to see the nuns. Thérèse remembered so vividly the times she and Papa had come to pray here during their afternoon walks. First the grille had taken Pauline. Then Marie. What was behind that grate? What was so mysterious and exciting? As the years passed, and much too slowly at that, Thérèse began to realize the beauty of the life Pauline and Marie had chosen. At the heart of their vocation was a person, the person of Jesus. What a marvelous call they had received: to be brides of Christ.

Thérèse's eyes met the gaze of Mother Genevieve, who was in adoration before the Blessed Sacrament. Thérèse knelt next to her for a moment and experienced the awareness that she was with a saint. Mother Genevieve of St. Thérèse, who lived from 1805 until 1891, had founded the Lisieux Carmel in 1838. In *Story of a Soul,* Thérèse wrote: "I remained kneeling for a moment at her feet, thanking God for the grace he gave me of knowing a saint..." *(Story).* Then Thérèse left the choir and followed Mother Marie de Gonzague on a tour of the monastery. She felt an excitement fused with peace and calm. Thérèse joined in the rhythm of monastic life. While everything was new, and nothing for her could be considered routine, still her approach to the daily living out of her decision to enter Carmel reflected a maturity beyond her years. She felt that she had a realistic grasp of what her life would consist of for as long as she would live. "I found the religious life to be *exactly* as I had imagined it." She found more thorns than roses. "Yes," she said, "suffering opened wide its arms to me and I threw myself into them with love" *(Story).* Thérèse felt that the Lord was calling her to suffer for the spiritual needs of those for whom he died. She was especially sensitive to the Carmelite vocation to pray for priests. As she began her life at Carmel, the young postulant made sure to keep her sufferings to herself. She was determined that the sisters would not be able to detect a tear or a frown. She was serene.

Sister Marie's Profession

Thérèse's oldest sister, Marie of the Sacred Heart, pronounced her vows on May 22, 1888, while her youngest sister was still new to religious life. Father Almire Pichon, S.J., came for the profession ceremony. Much earlier in Thérèse's *Story of a Soul* she referred to the torment she had carried in her heart for about five years, from the time of her mysterious illness at age ten to Sister Marie's profession. Father Pichon had helped the new postulant to make a general confession. He listened compassionately as Thérèse poured out her weaknesses and sins. She tried earnestly to be as sincere as she could. Most of all, she seemed to have felt the nagging guilt that she could have possibly been responsible for her own illness as a child of ten. Father Pichon grasped the anxiety in Thérèse's soul. He could see her sincerity and desire to grow and mature in the spiritual life. But Thérèse does recall that Father Pichon considered her fervor to be childish and her spiritual journey very sweet. Speaking of her confession to Father Pichon, Thérèse writes: "...the Father of our souls, as with a wave of his hand, removed all my doubts. Since then I am perfectly calm" *(Story)*. At the end of her confession, Father Pichon assured her that she had never committed a mortal sin. He said: "Thank God for what He has done for you; had he abandoned you, instead of being a little angel, you would have become a little demon.... My child, may Our Lord always be your superior and your novice master" *(Story)*. These last words deeply moved Thérèse and she would later note that Jesus was her only spiritual director. Father Pichon was transferred to Canada in 1888. Thérèse had considered him to be her spiritual director, so his transfer was a disappointment. Just the same, Thérèse wrote to him every month. Father Pichon answered her correspondence with one letter a year. He really had left her to the Lord, the perfect novice master.

The Way Grows Steep and Rocky

Thérèse had no *illusions* about the challenges of the day to day living out of religious life. It was not going to be easy, but she wasn't asking for an easy life. She believed suffering to be an inevitable part of the human condition, a Christian's sharing in the cross of Jesus. She was no stranger to conflict and suffering. Although she had grown up in a loving family environment, she had gone to a boarding school where she had experienced her share of pains as well as some happy times, too. Thérèse realized that the Lord's invitation to holiness could be found through her loving acceptance of a sharp word, an impatient glance, an insinuating remark.

Although she had been Papa's *little queen* at *Les Buissonnets,* she was not a *queen* at Carmel. In those early convent days, when difficulties arose, Thérèse must have been tempted to run to Pauline and Marie who were like mothers to her. But she did not permit herself to do this. She forced herself to adhere to the rules and protocol of her Order because she believed that the Lord wanted this sacrifice of her.

Mother Marie de Gonzague had accepted Thérèse willingly into Carmel. When Thérèse was just nine years old, Mother de Gonzague had said that Thérèse had a vocation to Carmel, although she would have to wait until she was sixteen. Although the prioress could be delightful and gracious with Thérèse, she could also be very stern. Thérèse admits that during her postulancy, she couldn't meet Mother de Gonzague without having to kneel down and kiss the floor for some mistake or infraction of the Rule. Thérèse recalls the cobweb she missed while sweeping the dimly-lit hallway. If she would have lived in the days of electricity, Thérèse would no doubt have seen the cobweb and have been spared some humiliation. But this was not the case. In front of all the nuns, Mother de Gonzague said: "We can easily see that our cloisters are swept by a child of fifteen! Go and take that cobweb away and be more careful in the future" *(Story).* Thérèse recognized that she often displeased the prioress. She realized that she was very slow in completing her duties. The cobweb was a clue that she should aim to become more thorough. But Thérèse was perplexed. It was helpful to be *told,* but she wanted to be *shown* how to improve. This was what her novice mistress did.

Being corrected occasionally in front of the community was humiliating, but another challenge hurt more. The novice mistress, Sister Marie of the Angels, sent Thérèse daily during nice weather to weed the convent garden. The novice mistress was "really a saint," according to Thérèse. Sister Marie of the Angels must have realized how much a new postulant would appreciate being outdoors among the flowers and shrubs. That part of the assignment was delightful. The other side of the coin was that Mother de Gonzague usually passed by in late afternoon. It was inevitable that Thérèse would meet her. The postulant records in her *Story of a Soul* some biting words from the prioress: "Really, this child does nothing at all! What sort of novice has to take a walk every day?" The treatment Thérèse received from Mother de Gonzague in no way resembled the gentle compassion of her father and sisters. But as difficult as their relationship became, Thérèse reflected a profound understanding of the mother prioress and a sincere love for her.

Spiritual Life at Carmel

Within the Carmelite Order of Thérèse's era, two basic approaches to the spiritual life coexisted: *mystical* spirituality and *ascetical* spirituality. *Mystical* spirituality, as lived by St. John of the Cross and other great mystics, held *love* to be the essence of the spiritual life. It focused on God primarily as *Love*. Mother Genevieve, the foundress of the Lisieux Carmel, lived this spirituality. Along with her, Mother Agnes of Jesus, Thérèse's own sister and Thérèse herself were at home in that spiritual ambiance. The other approach to the spiritual life, the ascetical spirituality, predominated in Thérèse's time. The *ascetical* thrust was to see God primarily as a *judge*. According to this tradition, a person's spiritual focus was on making reparation, saving souls, performing extraordinary penances. Mother Marie de Gonzague favored this approach to the spiritual life.

Mother de Gonzague was simply herself. She walked through the pages of Thérèse's life causing a flurry at times, and yet the focus of the story remains, Thérèse, who demonstrates that she could learn positive lessons from everyone she met. Thérèse also shows us how she was genuinely grateful for the good done her and truly forgiving of those who hurt and insulted her.

As the days of Thérèse's postulancy passed, adjusting to her new life was not the only challenge. Papa's health was deteriorating rapidly. On June 23, 1888, he became disoriented and wandered away from home. While his Carmelite daughters prayed, Céline and Uncle Guerin searched for Mr. Martin. They found him on June 27 in La Havre. On August 12, Mr. Martin had another stroke, this time at *Les Buissonnets*. On October 31, Mr. Martin suffered still another serious relapse. His recovery was slow, but steady.

Mr. Martin's heart was set on visiting his daughters at Carmel. He was determined to be there on January 10, 1889, when his *little queen* would receive the religious habit. Nothing would keep him away—not even a legion of strokes.

11

The Bride

From January 5 through January 10, 1889, Thérèse prepared for the day on which she would receive the religious
habit of Carmel. She tried to keep her mind focused on the
seriousness of her retreat, but her heart fluttered with excitement just the same. Papa would be present to share her
joy as he had always been there for her in the happy times,
in the sad times, in the everyday times. It seemed for so long
that Papa might not recover, but he did, and he would be
there, the proud father, to give his Thérèse away.

Bishop Hugonin would officiate, which would add so-
lemnity to the ceremony. Thérèse smiled as she remembered what she had gone through, what Papa had gone
through, and for that matter, what the bishop had gone
through to enable her to follow her call. Thérèse had not
received her wish to enter Carmel for Christmas, 1887, but
she realized in time that the three month delay had been
spiritually enriching. In fact, she said that March, 1888, had
been "One of the most beautiful months of my life" *(Story)*.

Thérèse had learned to wait and to deepen her trust in
the Lord.

Clothing Day

It was Bishop Hugonin who selected January 10, 1889
as the day for Thérèse's reception of the habit. On that

same day Thérèse would begin the next stage of her religious formation: the novitiate. The evening before, she gazed out of the monastery window. The courtyard was gray and barren. A light drizzle was falling. Thérèse's imagination traveled to the chapel which would look so bright and festive the next day; then back to the cloister courtyard—a bleak patch of earth in the misty shadows.

Thérèse thrilled to think that she would be surrounded by Papa and her sisters, as well as by the Guerins, at the ceremony. Could she possibly ask the Lord for one more little favor? And for him, the Lord of heaven and earth, it would truly be a *little* favor. It didn't hurt to ask. Snow, if only she could have snow.

The mild weather continued the next morning. Thérèse had to admit that snow would be highly unlikely, but that was fine too. The celebration was here and she felt excited and happy. Dressed in her bridal gown and veil, Thérèse's sandy curls hugged the rim of the veil's crown then fell in natural ringlets to her shoulders. Her pink cheeks glowed, a combination of robust health and excitement. Her deep-set eyes were alert, anxious to see her *king of France and Navarre.*

It was time for Thérèse to step out of the cloister into the entrance where Mr. Martin and the family waited. Papa's eyes shone as he hugged his youngest daughter. How proud he was of her, so grown up, so in love with her calling. Mr. Martin seemed once again to be his old self. The strokes were forgotten. He felt today like the much younger father he had once been when he and Thérèse had taken their daily afternoon strolls, visiting local churches to adore the Blessed Sacrament. Happy memories crowded his mind—the Sunday walks to Mass when little Thérèse had clung proudly to his hand, the family recreations before the fireplace.

Today Thérèse's lips smiled while her eyes shimmered with tears. She was happy and sad, laughing and crying all at once. How she had missed Papa, yet now he was here, for this wonderful though brief occasion. The bishop was ready. It was time to begin. Thérèse took Papa's arm so simply and surely. The *king* patted her hand affectionately. Together they walked down the aisle, slowly, in step. Papa beamed and Thérèse looked modestly up at him. The joy on his face was transparent. The sisters sang and Bishop Hugonin moved the ceremony reverently ahead.

Thérèse was reflecting on Papa's generosity with God. He had given all his children to the Lord. Céline had recently confided to her father her desire to enter Carmel. Léonie, too, was convinced of her religious vocation. She would just take longer to settle into her life as a Visitation nun. All his children were a consolation for Papa. But Thérèse was a realist. Her father's health was precarious. Today could be considered, in comparison to Jesus' life on earth, as the Palm Sunday triumph before the Passion. Thérèse felt as if pain and humiliation, caused by the weight of his illness, were stalking her father. Whatever suffering Papa would bear would be just as much her suffering, and that of her sisters. If only she could spare him the least amount of grief. If only she could take his sickness upon her own healthy shoulders. But that would be up to her Spouse. There was a king even more powerful than the *king of France and Navarre*. Papa and Thérèse were convinced of that.

At the conclusion of the celebration the bishop introduced an unplanned addition. He solemnly intoned the *Te Deum,* a hymn of thanksgiving to God usually sung when the religious pronounced their vows.

After the ceremony, Thérèse left chapel and embraced her father. He was tired, but at peace. Thérèse's eyes followed him as he slipped out of the door onto the walkway with the other relatives. The young nun's eyes burned as she reentered the cloister and came face to face with the prominent statue of the Child Jesus. Could it be smiling only at her? Papa's departure seemed to settle more peacefully in her heart. Then an unusual brightness caught Thérèse's eye. She glanced beyond the statue into the cloister garden. It was completely covered with snow!

Bishop Hugonin came into the cloister after the ceremony and visited with the community. He liked Thérèse, as she records in her *Story of a Soul.*

She explained that the bishop told everyone "I was '*his* little girl.'" The priests who had accompanied the bishop now heard recounted the story of Mr. Martin and Thérèse's trip to the bishop's residence in Bayeux. Bishop Hugonin enthusiastically described the way Thérèse had piled her hair on top of her head to look older. Thérèse felt her cheeks blush. She enjoyed the mirth, even if it was at her expense. Thérèse notes that during another visit to Carmel, Bishop Hugonin "took my head in his hands and gave me a thousand caresses" *(Story)*. She recognized the bishop's kindness to be a consolation from her Spouse. When the guests had gone and the cloister resumed its normal routine, Thérèse reviewed the events of the day, the meaning of the ceremony, the presence of Papa, the kindness of the bishop and the snow. All were like a cluster of beautiful gifts from the Lord.

Just a month later, on February 12, 1889, Mr. Martin's condition worsened. He became disoriented and had to be hospitalized at *Bon Sauveur,* a mental institution in Caen, France. Léonie and Céline boarded at St. Vincent de Paul orphanage to be near their father and visit him daily. Thérèse and her sisters at Carmel attended to their religious life while feeling the intense pain of their father and two sisters in Caen.

Mr. Martin lived at *Bon Sauveur* for three years. Thérèse took upon herself his suffering and humiliation. As she tidied the refectory and swept the corridors, she offered her actions for Papa, for priests, for those who suffered in any way. During her stay in Caen, Céline's relationship with the Lord grew. With that growth came a real desire to follow her sisters to Carmel. Her letters became hymns of confidence in the Lord. When she came to visit Carmel, she and Thérèse shared trusting spiritual conversations. The rest of 1889 passed uneventfully.

Preparing for the Vowed Life

During 1889 Thérèse was a novice. She was given the opportunity to deepen her understanding of the spirituality, the history and the lifestyle of the Carmelite Order. As a religious she would profess three vows of poverty, chastity and obedience, according to the spiritual heritage of the Carmelite tradition. Her novice mistress, Sister Marie of the Angels, was particularly gentle. Thérèse's novitiate days, for the most part, were serene. She entrusted her concern for Papa to Jesus and poured her energy into spending each day, each moment, doing what she felt the Lord was calling her to do at that specfiic time.

A few small things could have temporarily caused her to lose her peace of mind. On one occasion, in the evening, during the time of the *grand silence*, Thérèse filed out of chapel to the closet where the sisters kept their oil lamps. A lamp served as each sister's only source of light, illuminating her small cell until the rising of the sun the next morning. When Thérèse, at the end of the line, approached the shelf, her lamp was gone. She searched and felt along the edges. The shelf was empty. Thérèse was annoyed at first. It wasn't fair. Each sister had a lamp assigned to her. To take someone else's was unjust. But as

Thérèse inched her way along the dark hallway to her room, she began to relax and think about the incident. After all, she reflected, she was preparing herself to take a vow of poverty out of love for Jesus. Poverty, she realized in that moment, could embrace not only the useful things, but even the essential. And if she could find serenity when suffering real inconvenience, she could also find an opportunity to grow. "And so in this *exterior darkness,* I was interiorly illumined," Thérèse explained *(Story).*

When she had just entered Carmel, Postulant Thérèse still preferred pretty things whenever she had the opportunity to have or use them. But as time went on, Thérèse made it a point to choose what was plain or less convenient. She never made any fuss about this, nor did she give an explanation for her unlikely choices. This was the kind of hidden gift, so small in her own estimation, that she could offer to Jesus as an act of love. When someone went into her cell, removed her delicate water jug and left a large chipped one in its place, she smiled and said nothing. Such small spiritual acts were countless. Thérèse liked to offer them for Papa, for her family, for priests and religious, for the people who asked for the nuns' prayers, for prisoners. She kept present in her mind all in mission lands who still waited to hear the Gospel. Thérèse prayed and performed her duties for missionaries, that they would have the energy, the courage and the love of God to be equal to their challenging vocation.

As Thérèse prepared water pitchers before meals and put the dining area in order after each meal, she saw the faces of those who were counting on her prayers. She believed that what she did had value in the Church because of the infinite love and mercy of Jesus. She prayed and offered sacrifices for the suffering souls in purgatory as well. The actions of her life were so ordinary, yet she trusted that the infinite love of Jesus could consider the smallest action as a hymn of praise. The walls of Thérèse's monastery were the boundaries through which she would penetrate the world with the love she asked of the Lord.

How many times during that novitiate year she must have remembered her pilgrimage to Rome. At this time particularly she could have remembered her train ride through Switzerland: the plush green hills, the valleys and meadows reflecting the bright sun, rippling springs dancing down the hillside and, in the background, the breathtaking mountains and deep gorges. She remembered the little towns nestled in the mountainsides along the way. Thérèse had sat glued to the window of the train. The passing view had been like a scene out of a picture book and it remained engraved in her memory. She remembered how she had reflected on her vocation to Carmel as the train wound through the mountains. "I understood how easy it is to become all wrapped up in self, forgetting entirely the sublime goal of one's calling. I said to myself: When I am a prisoner in Carmel and trials come my way and I have only a tiny bit of the starry heavens to contemplate, I shall remember what my eyes have seen today. This thought will encourage me and I shall easily forget my own little interests..." (Story).

Hidden Victories

Thérèse realized how easy it is for people to excuse their weaknesses and mistakes. Just as easy was it to want to look good, to appear virtuous, to be esteemed. Who could be comfortable realizing that they were not well thought of by the community? Thérèse's sensitive nature caused her to do battle with herself. She emphasized hidden simplicity, although her natural desire to want to shine posed a constant challenge. An example of being misunderstood is recorded in *Story of a Soul*. The novice mistress had found a small broken vase that had fallen from the windowsill. No one had offered any explanation, nor even bothered to pick up the pieces. The novice mistress gathered the pieces of the vase and approached Thérèse. She showed it to the novice and admonished her to be more careful. Thérèse's cheeks burned. She longed to tell the nun that she had not done it. But in that moment between choices, Thérèse considered. She chose not to offer an excuse or guess an explanation. Instead, she thanked the novice mistress, and as was the custom, she bent low, kissed the floor and promised to be more careful in the future.

On certain occasions Thérèse approached Mother de Gonzague for spiritual direction. Thérèse was thirsty for guidance, being still so new to religious life. However the prioress spent a significant portion of their hour together scolding her for what seemed to be imperfections. The experience was not pleasant but Thérèse realized that it was a blessing in its own way. She could not be drawn to any human attachment for the prioress she had known since she was a child. At the end of Thérèse's novitiate year, Mother de Gonzague told her that her profession of vows would be delayed for another eight months. Thérèse does not elaborate, but her age was most probably the reason. She would have just turned seventeen at the time. Whether she anticipated this setback or not, she doesn't say. Rather, her focus was on finding serenity amidst the unexpected and readying herself for profession day.

Giving Up Pauline Again

During her novitiate, Thérèse spent a good deal of time attending to the dining area and related duties. Another nun was also assigned to the task: Pauline. Thérèse was thrilled to be able to work alongside the sister whom she called her *second mother*. But the Rule did not permit them to speak to one another. Thérèse longed to sit for just a little while and pour out her concerns to Pauline, the way she had at *Les Buissonnets*. To forego this consolation was the most difficult sacrifice of all. She had been so free at home. Now she had the gift of her independence to offer the Lord.

Eight months passed by. Thérèse's profession was set for September 8, 1890. Bishop Hugonin planned to officiate. Céline felt that Papa was well enough to travel by carriage from Caen. Papa would not be able to stay for the entire ceremony, but Céline had thought of how to handle it. She and Papa would arrive toward the end and Papa would go up to the grille so that he could give Thérèse his blessing.

Profession Day

The evening before profession found Thérèse in inner turmoil. This was her first bout with temptations about her vocation to religious life, to Carmel. Her life in the monastery flashed before her. The whole thing seemed like a mistake, a ridiculous mistake. She wanted to have a vocation to Carmel, but probably was not called. By being there she was doing her own will, not God's, the one thing she feared more than anything. What had she been thinking of? How could she have been so blind? She paced the floor of her little cell, trying to find peace. But it was useless. The serenity she had so often touched had been replaced by a raging storm. She couldn't go ahead with the ceremony the next day. She had to get help.

Thérèse sought out the novice mistress and asked to speak with her. The novice's tormented expression spoke more eloquently than words. The novice mistress understood at once what Thérèse was going through. It was a temptation, she assured her. She could go ahead with profession without any more preoccupation. Thérèse felt peace flood her soul again. She went to find the prioress and confided the whole episode to her. As she told her story, Mother de Gonzague laughed softly. She too, believed that the doubt was only a temptation.

The sky on the morning of September 8 was bright and cloudless. Thérèse was ready to pronounce her vows. Papa was unable to make the trip, even if only to arrive at the end of the ceremony. Deprived of the presence of her earthly father, Thérèse realized she could truly pray the words of the Lord's Prayer: "Our Father who art in heaven." Thérèse pronounced her vows joyfully. Close to her heart she carried a handwritten letter which read:

O Jesus, my Divine Spouse!
May I never lose the second robe of my baptism.
Take me before I can commit the slightest voluntary fault.
May I never see nor find anything but Yourself alone.
May creatures be nothing for me, and may I be
     nothing for them,
but may you, Jesus, be everything!
May the things of earth never be able to trouble my soul,
and may nothing disturb my peace.
Jesus, I ask you for nothing but peace, and also love,
infinite love without any limits other than yourself;
love which is no longer I but you, my Jesus.
Jesus, may I die a martyr for you.
Give me martyrdom of heart or of body, or rather
     give me both.
Give me grace to fulfill my vows in all their perfection,
and make me understand what a real spouse should be.
Never let me be a burden to the community,
let nobody be occupied with me,
let me be looked upon as trampled underfoot,
forgotten like your little grain of sand, Jesus.
May your will be done in me perfectly,
and may I arrive at the place you have prepared for me.
Jesus, allow me to save very many souls;
let no soul be lost today;
let all the souls in purgatory be saved.

Jesus, pardon me if I say anything I should not say.
I want only to give you joy and to console you *(Story)*.

The ceremony in which Thérèse would receive the veil
was set for September 24, 1890. Thérèse looked forward
with delight to having Bishop Hugonin and Papa there.
Neither could come. Bishop Hugonin was ill and Papa was
too weak to travel. Humanly speaking, it was a sad day for
Thérèse. She cried and noted that her tears were misunderstood. Still, Jesus had permitted this. He left her
without special graces on that day. Without his help, she
admitted, she could do nothing but cry.

12

Serving the God of Peace

From October 8 through the 15, 1891, Father Alexis Prou, a Franciscan from Caen, preached an annual retreat to the nuns of the Lisieux Carmel. Thérèse had made a novena to prepare herself well. She did not always find preached retreats practical for her particular life situation. Besides, she had heard that Father Alexis' "specialty" was reconciling great sinners with the Church. After the retreat master had spoken just a few words, Thérèse received the grace to understand that this priest would help her to grow in the spiritual life as much as if Jesus himself were guiding the retreat. Thérèse felt that Father Alexis understood her. She wrote later: "He launched me full sail upon the waves of confidence and love which so strongly attracted me, but upon which I dared not advance" *(Story).* The other sisters did not draw the same insights from the retreat homilies. Thérèse was convinced that the Lord had given her a singular invitation to proceed on the way of love. In fact, she was the only one who truly appreciated that retreat. Thérèse deepened her penetration of the power of love as a means to progress rapidly in the spiritual life. She realized initially that love alone had the capacity to help her overcome her natural fears and timidity. Love gave her the strength to soar.

Mother Genevieve's Legacy

Thérèse admired the elderly nun propped up in the infirmary bed. Mother Genevieve, foundress of the Lisieux Carmel, had become holy, Thérèse felt, by practicing hidden, ordinary virtues. Thérèse stopped in, intending to stay only a moment because two sisters were already visiting. The Rule permitted only two at a time. As the young sister backed away, Mother Genevieve offered her a thought or *spiritual bouquet:* "Serve God with *peace* and *joy;* remember, my child, *our God is a God of peace*" *(Story).* Thérèse had been having a difficult day. Mother Genevieve's words lifted her spirits immediately.

On the following Sunday, Thérèse went again to the infirmary to visit. Thérèse had thought about Mother's wise advice during that week and asked if what she had said had been a revelation. The old nun assured Thérèse that the message had come from her, not from any extraordinary intervention.

Thérèse remembered how she had gone to visit Mother Genevieve on her profession day. The young sister had manifested the terrible temptation she had done battle with the night before she had pronounced her vows. Mother Genevieve explained that she too had gone through a similar trial before professing her vows.

Thérèse was one of the sisters who assisted Mother Genevieve during her final hours on this earth. On December 5, 1891, the elderly nun was near death. Thérèse was positioned at the foot of the bed, facing Mother. A kind of numbness took over as Thérèse watched and prayed. Time ticked slowly by. Just before Mother Genevieve passed into eternity, Thérèse experienced joy filling her whole being. She felt fervent, encouraged in her vocation. Thérèse remembered at that moment that once she had told Mother Genevieve that she would never see purgatory. Mother had replied simply that she hoped not.

After her death, the sisters prayed and mourned in silence at her bedside. Then each slipped away. Several took some small token of remembrance, some small relic. Thérèse's relic was unique. When Mother Genevieve was laid out in the choir, Thérèse waited until no one was around. She moved closer and taking a small piece of linen cloth collected one lone tear that still glistened on the dead nun's eyelid. That tear was for Thérèse and she felt that it was a tear of joy. Soon after, Thérèse had a dream. The elderly nun was making out her will and dispensing her treasures to the community of sisters gathered around her. Thérèse being one of the youngest was last. She felt preoccupied because Mother Genevieve would have nothing left to give her. But the dream led to a wonderful surprise. Thérèse stood in front of Mother Genevieve who smiled at her and said three times: "To you I give my heart" *(Story)*. When Thérèse woke up, she remembered the incident vividly.

Influenza at Carmel

On Thérèse's nineteenth birthday, Sister St. Joseph, the oldest member of the community, died. It was January 2, 1892. Two other sisters also died: Sr. Magdalene and Sister Febronie, the mother subprioress. Thérèse found Sister Magdalene dead in her cell. She hastened to the sacristy and returned to place a wreath of roses on Sister Magdalene's head. Then Thérèse sought help. As the influenza worked its course, Thérèse and two others were the only nuns still standing. They served the community and tried to take care of each one's needs. Sister St. Stanislaus, the head sacristan, was also in bed and was very ill. Thérèse took care of the sacristy and arranged all of the details of the funeral of each of the nuns. In *Story of a Soul*, Thérèse wrote pensively, "It is impossible to imagine the sad state of the community at this time." Yet, she was able to find reason to be joyful even in the midst of that trial. Through it all, she was given permission to receive communion every day. She was also pleased to be able, as temporary sacristan, to touch and care for the sacred vessels used by the priest for the celebration of Mass.

Despite the consolations, Thérèse often felt drowsy and distracted during prayer times. After communion, as she struggled to pray with fervor, Thérèse resolved to continue her thanksgiving throughout her day. One morning she wondered if the Lord could possibly be pleased with her. She asked for a little sign. If he was upset, would he let the priest give her just half a host at communion time? Thérèse's turn came to receive the Holy Eucharist. She watched as the priest took two hosts and placed them reverently on her tongue.

Pauline: My Living Jesus

Sister Agnes of Jesus, Thérèse's second oldest sister Pauline, was elected prioress of the Lisieux Carmel on February 20, 1893. She was appointed for a three-year term. Five years after Thérèse's death, on April 19, 1902, Mother Agnes was again elected prioress. In 1923, Pope Pius XI, who beatified and canonized Thérèse, confirmed Mother Agnes as prioress of the Lisieux Carmel for life. She died on July 28, 1951, at the age of ninety.

Thérèse was overjoyed that Pauline was appointed prioress, but she was subdued in her jubilation, out of sensitivity for the feelings and preferences of the others. The youngest of the Martins looked up to Pauline and learned to read the book of Jesus in her life. Thérèse understood her sister's sensitive heart and saw the inevitable daily crosses and contradictions Pauline endured. Thérèse noted the tranquillity of her older sister, a tranquillity she recognized to be the fruit of suffering accepted for the love of Jesus. It was the Lord himself who had unfolded the mysteriously charming quality of suffering to the *little queen*. Her memory flashed back to the boarding school where she had fumbled along to mingle with her peers. Who had understood her there in the early adolescent years? Only Jesus, who waited for her in the silence of the tabernacle. And she had felt accepted by him, drawn to his heart, confident that he loved her. It was like Papa's love stretched to the infinite. Now, thinking back to the loneliness and pain, Thérèse reflected that these tools brought her closer to Jesus. The very same tools were at work in Pauline's life to make her religious life rich and fruitful, not only for her, but for the people who counted on her prayers and sacrificial lifestyle. "Very truly, I tell you, unless a grain of wheat falls into the earth and dies, it remains just a single grain; but if it dies, it bears much fruit" (Jn 12:24).

As Thérèse continued her day-to-day life at Carmel, she reflected on her desires and motivations. She was in awe of Pauline's talents for painting and composing poetry. Thérèse saw these talents offered to Jesus for his glory as something wonderful. She thought of how pleasing they must be to the Lord. But although she felt strongly drawn to pursue painting or the writing of poetry herself, she would never ask permission to follow the inclination. Why should she seek good things unless the Lord wanted them for her? She reflected on the words of Ecclesiastes: "Then I considered all that my hands had done and the toil I had spent in doing it, and again, all was vanity and a chasing after wind, and there was nothing to be gained under the sun" (Eccl 2:11).

Thérèse was astonished when she too was given the opportunity to develop her talents for painting and writing poetry, but she was in peace about it as well because she had not asked or manifested her desire for these. It was the Lord's gift to her because she had tried to remain humble. She also learned that gifts and talents do not take one away from God unless one forgets the Source of the gifts. When the receiver recognizes the divine Giver, the very recognition serves to draw that person closer to God.

The Best for My King

From the date he was released from *Bon Sauveur* in 1892, until his death two years later, Louis Martin visited Carmel only once. Céline and Uncle Guerin helped the frail old man as he stepped into the monastery entrance. How familiar this building was to him. When Papa was leaving he looked upward for a long time and said aloud with feeling: "In heaven." Thérèse gazed at Papa until his figure had burned itself into her memory. She would never forget the details of this visit which was to be her father's last. Mr. Martin died on July 29, 1894. He was seventy years old.

Mr. Martin's death and Céline's entrance into Carmel are closely linked. A few months after her father's death, Céline became the fourth Martin sister to join the Carmel of Lisieux. It was September 14, 1894. Thérèse and her sisters were jubilant.

From the day Thérèse had entered Carmel, April 9, 1888, until Céline actually entered the Order, the youngest of the Martins had prayed for her sister. Thérèse suffered to think of the temptations that the world threw at her. Céline, considered by Thérèse as "my other self," was precious to her. Although Thérèse could have accepted and respected Céline's decision to choose another calling or another Order, she was convinced that Céline's place was at Carmel. This was her prayer, her hope that she took to the feet of her Spouse.

There were obstacles of course. When the community was consulted about the possibility of accepting Céline into the Order, one of the senior members objected strenuously. She felt that three sisters from the same family was sufficient for a community of about twenty nuns. Sister Aimee of Jesus was convinced and there seemed no changing of her mind.

Thérèse was praying her thanksgiving after communion one morning. She had two particular intentions: could the Lord in his goodness convince Sister Aimee to reverse her decision, thus removing the obstacle to Céline's entrance into Carmel? The second: would the Lord do this wonderful thning as a sign that Papa was in heaven with God? With childlike trust, Thérèse prayed and believed that she would receive a sign. She wanted to know that her father was not in purgatory, but in eternal bliss. After all, at her request the Lord had moved the hardened sinner, Henri Pranzini, to repentance moments before his execution, Thérèse also had been given snow the morning she received her religious habit. She had even been able to find in theGarden of Carmel her favorite wildflower, the corn cockle. If Jesus was willing to take care of major and minor details in her life to please his beloved, wouldn't he take care of these most important matters: Papa's eternal happiness and Céline's vocation? Yes, Thérèse believed he would. She rose and left the choir.

Someone was waiting in the shadows. Thérèse was startled for a moment, but then quickly identified the figure. It was Sister Aimee of Jesus. Thérèse managaed a feeble smile. "Could we speak for a moment?" the older nun asked, pointing to a nearby room. Tears filled Sister Aimee's eyes as she struggled to find the words. At last she said softly, "I have changed my mind about my opposition to Céline's entrance into Carmel." Thérèse was ecstatic. This was better than snow, better than her favorite flower. This pertained to the most precious gifts of life: salvation and sanctification. Together, Sister Aimee and Sister Thérèse went to tell Mother Agnes of Jesus the wonderful news. Thérèse recognized with gratitude the graces the Lord was granting her. She was at peace about Papa and Céline. Céline, the object of so many prayers, entered in September of 1894. She was given the name Sr. Genevieve of the Holy Face.

Love Alone Attracts Me

In writing her spiritual journey, *Story of a Soul,* Thérèse explained the way she could see herself being directed by Jesus. Other attractions such as the desire to suffer and to die for Jesus lost their appeal. She was led to understand that the most important treasure of all is *love* and the way to obtain it is *abandonment to God* in everything. "Now, abandonment alone guides me," she wrote. "I have no other compass! I can no longer ask for anything with fervor except the accomplishment of God's will in my soul."

When she was seventeen and eighteen, Thérèse had read and found comfort in the mystical writings of the Carmelite Doctor of the Church, St. John of the Cross. But as time went on she drifted away from books, even the best of books. At this time, she focused her meditations and spiritual reading on two only: the *Bible* and *The Imitation of Christ.* She felt drawn to these books alone. She became convinced that Jesus was working in her soul without words. She felt that he was there throughout her day, enlightening her to understand and grasp situations, to choose wisely, to say and do what was right. From experience she realized that God's kingdom was within her.

Thérèse felt irresistibly attracted by the infinite mercy of God. She realized that the Lord was offering her many graces which convinced her that God should be loved, not feared. She saw love as the purifier and motivation for weak human beings. She felt that through love, "no one would ever consent to cause him any pain" *(Story)*. Thérèse saw all of God's perfection as rooted in *love,* even his justice. On June 9, 1895, while at Mass, Thérèse received the inspiration to offer herself to Merciful Love. Two days later, with the permission of Mother Agnes of Jesus, the prioress, Thérèse and Céline together made the Act of Oblation to Merciful Love.

Finding Jesus' Face in the Daily Trials

It wasn't that Thérèse had expected to find in Carmel an escape from the inevitable challenges of life. She had understood, young though she was, that her life would be tedious at times. She realized that in following her vocation to Carmel, she would have to find ways of helping herself to keep from turning in on herself and her own world. The unavoidable difficulties came. First of all, the austere lifestyle was challenging to a teenager who had experienced little hardship. The sisters rose at 5:30 A.M. and retired at 10:30 P.M. They came together to recite the Divine Office in the choir morning, mid-day and evening. They also spent two hours daily in private prayer. There were two periods of community recreation, after dinner and after supper. Breakfast was a very light meal; on fast days something to drink and a piece of dry bread. The remainder of the day was spent in doing household tasks or other manual work, always in silence and as much as possible in solitude.

Thérèse liked the community and blended in nicely. The painful days of her childhood spent on the fringes of loneliness at the Benedictine school were no more. Thérèse's outgoing personality, sensitive and cheerful, caused several of the Carmelites to value her presence and cherish her as a gift to the community. But there were challenges to face as well. Céline's testimony at the

Church's investigation into the holiness of Thérèse explains some of these and comments on the virtues Thérèse practiced in an heroic way.

Céline testified how she had confided to her sister that she found it difficult to be equally kind to all the sisters in community. Thérèse took the time to explain to Céline the importance of not showing preferences. In fact, Thérèse drew on an example from her own life. She mentioned by name a sister who was particularly annoying to her. Céline was astounded. She had seen Thérèse interacting with this sister. Thérèse was so kind and sensitive that Céline believed that this particular sister was one of Thérèse's closest friends.

Céline also confirmed that Thérèse longed for the practice of frequent holy communion, an uncommon practice before the papacy of St. Pius X (1903–1914). She so valued the importance of the reception of daily communion that she told the sisters she would take care of this matter from heaven. Thérèse promised Mother Marie de Gonzague that from heaven she would help her change her mind about the value of receiving communion frequently. After Thérèse's death what she had foretold actually happened. Mother Marie de Gonzague totally changed her thinking on the issue and asked the chaplains to offer the sisters the opportunity to receive communion every day.

13

Thérèse's Autobiography: a Mirror

Thérèse wrote the first part of her autobiography which has come to be known as *manuscript A* between 1895 and 1896 at the request of her sister Pauline, Mother Agnes, who was prioress at the time. It was entirely written during the limited free time which together with prayers and manual work comprised the monastic schedule. In this section of her autobiography she recreates events that struck Carmel, such as the influenza epidemic, as well as occasions of special significance to her, particularly her own profession of vows. Thérèse recounts the annual retreat preached by the Franciscan, Father Alexis, in which she felt her soul had been lifted onto the waves of hope and confidence. She also writes about her encounters with the saintly Mother Genevieve who had impressed her deeply, even recording the dream in which she received Mother Genevieve's heart.

Thérèse's pen captured the emotion of her Papa's death and the joy of Céline's entrance into Carmel. But Thérèse also apologized to Mother Agnes for having abbreviated the account of her own religious life.

Thérèse's sister, Léonie, was to leave the Visitation convent on July 20, 1895 and Marie Guerin, the Martin sisters' cousin, to enter Carmel on August 15. On October 17 of that same year Mother Agnes asked Thérèse to be a spiritual sister to Maurice Bellière, a seminarian and future missionary priest. On May 30, 1896, Mother Marie de Gonzague would give Thérèse a second spiritual brother, Adolphe Roulland, soon to be ordained as a priest of the Foreign Mission Society in Paris. All of these significant events are mentioned in Thérèse's autobiography.

On January 20, 1896, Thérèse took her copybook containing *manuscript A* to Mother Agnes. The matter seemed to die there as Mother Agnes placed it in a drawer and continued her busy days as prioress. On February 24, Céline, now Sister Genevieve, made her religious profession, receiving the veil on March 17. On the sameday, the Martins' cousin, Marie Guerin, received the habit. Thérèse was overjoyed by the double event.

On Saturday, March 21, 1896, the day before Passion Sunday, the Carmelites of Lisieux held their election for prioress. Sixteen of the sisters voted; the other eight prayed for the outcome according to God's will. Thérèse was among the eight who waited and prayed. When the election was final, the bell was rung and the entire community gathered in choir. Thérèse entered. The first thing she saw was Mother Marie de Gonzague in the chair of the prioress. Humanly speaking, it must have been a deep disappointment that her sister, Mother Agnes, had not been elected for another term. But Thérèse recognized the opportunity to trust in God and to see the prioress as the representative of Jesus. The momentary jolt she experienced subsided, and her little boat continued on its tranquil course. Thérèse's poetry sings the secrets of her soul and the reason for her serenity. Verse four of "Living on Love," dated February 26, 1895, explains:

> Living on Love is not setting up one's tent
> At the top of Tabor.
> It's climbing Calvary with Jesus,
> It's looking at the cross as a treasure!...
> In heaven I'm to live on joy.

Then trials will have fled forever,
But in exile, in suffering I want
To live on Love.
(*The Poetry of St. Thérèse of Lisieux*)

Thérèse did not fear the cross. She wanted to share the sufferings of her Spouse. With this disposition she had embraced the austere Carmelite Lenten fast with her usual youthful enthusiasm. The nuns remained in adoration before the Blessed Sacrament on the night between Holy Thursday and Good Friday. Thérèse had not obtained permission to do so and went to her room at midnight. She put out her oil lamp and retired. Just as her head rested on the pillow, Thérèse felt her mouth fill with warm fluid. She groped for her handkerchief and brought it to her lips. Could it be blood? Her first impulse was to check the handkerchief, but she had already extinguished her light. She decided to offer up the sacrifice of her curiosity to Jesus for someone in need. She would examine her handkerchief in the morning.

The bell sounded the time for rising. Thérèse drew back her window shutters and peered down at her handkerchief. It was stained with blood. She sought out Mother Marie de Gonzague to tell her. But Thérèse emphasized how well she felt and how much she wanted to continue the Lenten austerities. Mother clearly did not grasp the seriousness of Thérèse's condition and she consented. During the work periods that day, Thérèse cleaned the windows of the doors, helping to prepare the convent for the glory of Easter. During the evening of April 3, 1896, Thérèse had her second *hemoptysis* or hemorrhage. This was the sure sign of the presence of tuberculosis, a contagious disease of the lungs. In Thérèse's day, the medical profession offered home remedies to alleviate the patient's suffering, but there was no known cure. Thérèse was aware of that. Her main preoccupation centered on her

desire to carry out her community duties without inter-
ruption for as long as possible. That included the austere
penitential prayers and practices. She did not want to be
exempted from any of the rigors called for in daily convent
life. She saw fidelity to her duty and volunteering for extra
assignments as her little way to Jesus. This was her hymn of
love, not a glorious, magnificent hymn of the martyrs and
doctors of the Church, but a small, constant hymn awe-
some in its totality. On Easter Sunday, April 5, 1896,
Thérèse felt the joy of her risen Lord and harbored in her
heart the realization that she would soon enough be with
her Spouse forever.

From Good Friday, 1896 until her death on September 30, 1897, Thérèse walked the road to Calvary. Because her painful, bloody yet faithful journey is recorded
in her own *Story of a Soul* and the *Last Conversations* carefully written down by Mother Agnes, anyone who cares to
can approach her bedside and witness a saga of faith.
While Thérèse celebrated the joy of Easter, 1896, the
Lord soon after permitted her to be afflicted with a piercing gloom, a *dark night* in which she was tormented by
doubts against faith. It seemed to her that heaven was a
mirage, a fantasy. Beyond the grave was nothing. Thérèse
pictured the still body of her mother. She recalled how as
a child of four she had kissed the cold cheek. Where was
her mother? Where was her father? They were with God
in heaven, she knew it. She believed it. She mustered
every bit of energy to affirm her belief in God, in Jesus, in
the Creed, in eternal life. And even if she couldn't see or
have anything at all to cling to in this life, she would
never abandon the Lord. No matter how dark it seemed
to be with him at this time, to reject him would be the
greatest tragedy. Thérèse's face was serene. The anxiety
of her soul was never exteriorly manifested as she quietly
continued to follow the monastic schedule. She was the

assistant novice mistress during this period, and would remain such until that May. The novices never guessed, never even suspected, Thérèse's inner turmoil—a torment that would continue up until a few moments before her birth to new life.

Her Own Self on Paper

The next section of *Story of a Soul, manuscript B,* is dedicated to Thérèse's oldest sister, Sister Marie of the Sacred Heart of Jesus. The first part of *manuscript B* was written between September 13 and 16, 1896 and the second was written earlier, on September 8. In this section of the autobiography, Thérèse describes her spiritual insights about the *science of love* and her *little doctrine.* Although she was writing at the request of Sister Marie of the Sacred Heart, she wrote as if talking directly to Jesus.

Thérèse describes a dream in which she saw three nuns walking toward her. They were dressed in the distinctive Carmelite garb, mantles and long veils. She remembers that in her dream she longed to see the face of at least one of the Carmelites. As if in answer to her request, the tall sister in the middle lifted the veil which fell over her face and covered Thérèse with it. Thérèse knelt and felt overwhelmed with joy as she looked up into the face of Venerable Anne of Jesus. Thérèse recognized her as the foundress of the Carmelite Order in France. Mother Anne smiled at Thérèse with a heart filled with love. Because Venerable Anne was so approachable, Thérèse asked her with confidence if she would remain a long time on this earth or be with Jesus in heaven soon. The answer was *soon.* Thérèse asked if Jesus was pleased with her or if she should be doing something more for his glory. Mother Anne assured Thérèse that the Lord was contented with her. Just as she started to ask about her sisters, Thérèse woke up, but the joy lingered on.

Called to Be Love

After recalling the details of her dream, Thérèse continues to recount to Jesus in her *Story of a Soul* her awareness of the Lord's work in her soul. Six years had passed since she had made her profession of vows, years of rapid spiritual development and growth. Thérèse had a great heart. She wanted to respond to the Lord with her own small love in thanksgiving for the love he had extended to her. Her grateful prayer led her to desire to thank him by living out *all* the vocations in the Church. She wanted to be an apostle, a priest, a missionary, a martyr, a prophet, a doctor, whatever would bring the love of Jesus—that same love that had touched her life—to people. She realized that she was undeserving of the faith and of her Carmelite vocation. Nothing that she could do or say could merit those gifts that were beyond her capacity to acquire for herself. It was *Love* that had gifted her. It was *infinite Love* that gave value to every ministry in the Church. With her characteristic enthusiasm, Thérèse's imagination was hard at work. She saw the walls of her Carmelite convent come down brick by brick. Before the eyes of her soul lay the whole world. With St. Paul she wanted to be all to all. The great apostle had described the Christian meaning of *love*. Thérèse understood what Paul was saying. "I understood that Love comprised all vocations, that love was everything, that it embraced all times and places.... In a word, that it was eternal!

"Then, in the excess of my delirious joy, I cried out: O Jesus, my Love.... My *vocation*, at last I have found it.... My vocation is Love! Yes, I have found my place in the Church and it is You, O my God, who have given me this place; in the heart of the Church, my Mother, I shall be *Love*. Thus I shall be everything, and thus my dream will be realized" *(Story)*.

14

Challenges to Love

As she moved a day at a time toward eternity, young Thérèse mused about what was really important in life. She writes in her *Story of a Soul* about the tendency of human beings to let themselves be attached to the things of this earth. How easy it is, she admitted, to become distracted by the delights of this life and to forget God, the Source of all good. It was easier, of course, as a cloistered religious for Thérèse to be more detached from the things of this earth. She *had* less and she *saw* less. She had chosen this way of life as an act of love for Jesus.

But she wisely realized that even a nun could find ways to be attached to her own preferences. Thérèse wrote of concrete examples, such as the time when ideas that she had shared during recreation or in conversation with a sister were plagiarized by others. Something inside her naturally rebelled at the injustice. Yet if she were *truly* poor as her vow of poverty challenged her to be, she could not claim anything as her own, not even her clever ideas. Thérèse examined her heart on her relationships in community. She tried to honestly verify whether she was courageously striving to remove any spirit of competition. To guard against human tendencies that could block the work of the Holy Spirit in her, Thérèse deliberately chose to go against her preferences and inclinations. At community recreations, the sisters would enjoy each others' company. Some nuns were much more approachable and interesting. Thérèse would rarely seek them out. They had plenty of affection. She, instead, would focus her attention on those who were more withdrawn or harder to please. Thérèse saw herself as an artist's little brush to be used for the finishing touches on the canvas. Thérèse confides that the first time she, the little brush, could be used was in the postulancy. She and Martha were the two postulants. Although Martha was eight years older than Thérèse, the two quickly became good friends. The two friends were permitted to have spiritual conversations. At first, this was very enlightening to Thérèse. But as time passed, she noticed that things were changing. Their chats were more in line with the way worldly friends would share. Although younger, Thérèse realized it was her responsibility to speak up and suggest to her friend that the conversations be elevated to a spiritual plane. She also helped Martha to become aware of the challenge to overcome natural attachments to some sisters, even the prioress. It was necessary to keep one's heart rooted in the love of Jesus. Thérèse's friend was embarrassed at first, but then on reflection, she admitted the wisdom of Thérèse's advice and followed it. The two became even better friends in the true spirit of Carmel.

Thérèse battled her affectionate nature and overcame the desire to follow excuses that would bring her into contact and conversation with her two older sisters. She longed for the crumbs of human consolation, even just a word or a smile from Pauline and Marie. But the halls of Carmel were silent and empty.

Senior Novice

Even after her profession of vows, Thérèse asked for and received permission to remain in the novitiate where the atmosphere was stricter. From 1893 to 1896, she was asked to look after novitiate companions, helping them adjust to monastic life. In March, 1896, she became the acting novice mistress, a duty she carried out until May of 1897, although she never formally held the title.

Thérèse's own sister Céline became one of her novices. Céline admired her youngest sister's mature, sensitive manner and the ways in which Thérèse made herself available and helpful to the young women. Thérèse sought to know the novices and to guide and lead these lambs of Jesus to green pastures. With some novices she would be gentle, admitting how hard it was for her as well in a particular situation, or in the practice of a certain virtue. With other novices, Thérèse would be straightforward, almost blunt. She realized that she could not employ the gentle approach with sisters who could have seen admissions of struggle as weaknesses of character. "I know very well that your little lambs find me severe," she lamented to Jesus *(Story)*. Because Thérèse was not the actual novice mistress, some novices were rude and occasionally insulting to the young sister who went against the grain.

Other novices, however, were a delight. Thérèse tells of one who was her special charge. This sister had come from another Carmel. Her name was Sister Marie of the Trinity. One morning, at the beginning of Lent, 1895, Sister Marie approached Thérèse, her face radiant. She recounted her dream of the night before while Sister Thérèse listened intently. In her dream, Sister Marie was talking to her sister, a young woman who was very attracted to worldly living. The Carmelite was explaining stanza thirteen of a poem Sister Thérèse had recently written, entitled: "Living on Love." The particular words in the dream were:

"Loving you, Jesus, is such a fruitful loss!...

All my perfumes are yours forever" *(Story)*.

When she woke, the memory of the dream remained. Was it a sign that her sister might become a nun? Was it an invitation to Sister Marie to write to her sister suggesting that she consider the possibility of a religious vocation? Could she write to her sister as soon as Lent was over? Thérèse very kindly encouraged her to do so, but told her to first ask the prioress, which was the custom. The prioress was Pauline—Mother Agnes. No doubt Thérèse did not expect the reply Sister Marie received. Because Lent was still far from being over, Mother Agnes did not consider letterwriting a priority, even for such a worthy cause as encouraging a possible religious vocation. Mother responded that Carmelites saved souls, not through letters, but through prayer.

Thérèse interpreted this answer as the Lord's desire that she and Sister Marie of the Trinity pray for the young woman. They prayed ardently for the rest of Lent. As the feast of the resurrection brought renewed joy and hope, Sister Marie of the Trinity's sister did enter religious life and consecrated herself to Jesus. Sister Thérèse called this a miracle, attributed to the prayers of a believing novice who was humble enough to trust.

Sister St. Pierre

Pain was as familiar to Sister St. Pierre as her Carmelite calling. During the time when Thérèse was a novice, Sister St. Pierre was still able to maneuver her arthritic body to the choir and the refectory. During evening prayer before supper, she was directly in front of Thérèse. The novice had never experienced the kind of joint pain that plagued Sister St. Pierre, but she realized that the elderly nun was suffering. At ten to six each evening, Sister would shake her hourglass, signaling that it was time for her to begin her slow, careful walk to the community dining room. Someone would have to assist her to steady her steps. It was a volunteer situation and Thérèse wanted to be of service.

The old nun looked cautiously into the face of the young novice. What if Thérèse could not do it? What if she hurried or went too slow? What if she should fall? In the beginning, Thérèse experienced reluctance, even dread as the time approached. She knew she could never please the nun. It would be so easy to step back and let others try. They might be more capable, successful. But Thérèse went back with astounding regularity. She not only learned Sister St. Pierre's routine, she mastered it. Down the hall they went, making their way to the nun's seat in the dining room. Now Thérèse folded her sleeves back, careful not to hurt the twisted swollen hands. That was all that was required, but Thérèse realized that it was very hard for Sister St. Pierre to cut her bread. So Thérèse added this simple service. The elderly nun was completely won over.

One evening as they walked down the dimly lit corridor, Thérèse heard joyful music drifting through the cloister walls. She knew there must have been an elegant supper party going on in one of the nearby villas. Her imagination painted the bright rooms, plush furniture, a banquet and happy guests. She understood that this was not her life. Nor would it ever be. She looked into the face of Sister St. Pierre, then glanced around at the stark brick walls. How beautiful they seemed to her! She was where she belonged.

When Thérèse wrote her *Story of a Soul*, she recalled that she considered her daily walks with Sister St. Pierre a splendid opportunity to find Jesus in her suffering sister.

Lessons in Patience

Thérèse was assigned a seat in choir near a nun who made a strange little noise as she prayed and meditated. Thérèse described it as two sea shells being scraped together. Instead of letting the tension mount in her, Thérèse listened attentively and imagined that the irritating noise was really a lovely concert. In fact, it became a concert because Thérèse offered the sound to Jesus trusting that he could turn it into a symphony.

In the living of her ordinary daily life, Thérèse found the verses for her hymn of love.

15

On the Road to Calvary

Thérèse's illness progressed steadily. Her youthful energy was ebbing away. She poured all her strength into the performance of her daily tasks but eventually she could no longer go on. Still she pushed her pen across the page of her copybook to record her spiritual journey, as her superiors had asked of her.

"Ah! Mother," she wrote, "ever since I got sick, the cares you bestowed on me taught me a great deal about charity. No remedy appeared too expensive to you, and when it did not succeed you tried another thing without tiring. When I was going to recreation, what attention you paid in order to shelter me from drafts! Finally, if I wanted to tell all, I would never end.

"When thinking over all these things, I told myself that I should be as compassionate toward the spiritual infirmities of my sisters as you are, dear Mother, when caring for me with so much love" *(Story)*.

Thérèse reflected on various phrases of Scripture. She pondered the anxiety of Martha when Jesus visited her and her sister at Bethany. "It is not Martha's works that Jesus finds fault with.... It is only the *restlessness* of his ardent hostess that he willed to correct" *(Story)*. The last word she wrote with a pen was *restlessness*. She managed a few more paragraphs as she pushed her pencil doggedly ahead. The last words she recorded in her copybook were: "It is not because God, in his anticipating mercy, has preserved my soul from mortal sin that I go to him with confidence and love" *(Story)*.

In June of 1897 Thérèse was relieved of her convent duties. Her only remaining assignment was to complete the writing of her autobiography. She worked on it until July, spending much of her time outdoors in the garden in order to take advantage of the fresh air and sunshine. July 6 marked the beginning of a new stage in her illness. She began again to periodically vomit blood. This continued until August 5. On July 8, Thérèse was moved to the monastery infirmary where she would spend the remainder of her life. On that same day the statue of Mary, the Virgin of the Smile, was brought to her room. Thérèse could clearly see its serene face and she remembered vividly that Mary in this very statue had smiled at her when she was just ten years old. That smile of her heavenly mother had healed her.

The infirmary had a bed surrounded by curtains and a comfortable chair that she could sit in when she felt well enough. Thérèse pinned to the bed curtains her favorite holy pictures: "the Holy Face of Christ, the Blessed Virgin, her 'dear little' Theophane Venard, etc." *(Story)*. Theophane Venard was a young French missionary priest born in 1829. He had died a martyr in Hanoi, Indochina (now Hanoi, Vietnam). He was declared *blessed* by Pope Pius X on May 2, 1909, twelve years after the death of Thérèse, and declared a saint by Pope John Paul II in the group of saints called the Martyrs of Vietnam. Father Venard was the missionary whom Thérèse wanted to be in her desires, in her prayerfulness and self-sacrifice. She mentioned him often during the final stages of her illness.

Doctor de Corniere, the community's physician, stressed the seriousness of Thérèse's condition. The young nun felt like she was being wracked. Headaches and a piercing pain in her side tormented her. Frequently she felt she was suffocating and gasped frantically for air as the sweltering summer days bathed the small infirmary in humidity. The sisters adjusted her pillows and moved her gently in an effort to make her more comfortable. But there was little relief.

During the month of July, Thérèse had some intervals when she felt stronger. She manifested a cheerfulness that amazed the nuns who cared for her. The Anointing of the Sick was postponed because she did not seem sick enough. She was still able to carry on brief conversations with Mother Agnes (Pauline) and could answer her questions and the questions of her other two Carmelite sisters. Thérèse agreed that after her death some of her *remembrances* could be used for the information circular that would be sent to other Carmels. Gradually, cautiously, her sisters spoke about the eventual publication of her memoirs for everyone who wanted to read them. Thérèse did not oppose the idea, but she immediately entrusted the project to Mother Agnes. Of her autobiography, Thérèse said: "There will be something in it for all tastes, except for those in extraordinary ways" *(Conversations)*.

In the days that followed, Thérèse said mysterious things. "How unhappy I shall be in heaven if I cannot do little favors on earth for those whom I love...I will return! I shall come down!" *(Conversations)*

On July 17, 1897, Thérèse voiced the prediction that was to become not only famous but a marvelous source of consolation to countless people: "I especially feel that my mission is about to begin, my mission of making God loved as I love Him, of giving my little way to souls. If God answers my desires, my heaven will be spent on earth until the end of the world. Yes, I want to spend my heaven in doing good on earth" *(Conversations)*.

On July 28, Thérèse's condition worsened. It was an attack which she described as the beginning of "great sufferings." Doctor de Corniere announced that she would not live through the night. Quietly the sisters prepared an adjacent room with the things that would be needed for her burial. She received holy communion and the Anointing of the Sick. In Thérèse's time the Anointing of the Sick, called Extreme Unction, was administered only when a person was in immanent danger of death.

The long night of July 28 dawned quietly into the morning of July 29. As light slid through the window to announce another sultry day, Thérèse opened her eyes. She had survived the crisis. Thérèse was serene. The previous day she had expected to die. Now the doctor told her she had about a month to live. She said to Mother Agnes: "What does it matter if I remain a long time on earth? If I suffer very much and always more, I will not fear, for God will give me strength; he'll never abandon me" *(Conversations)*. Thérèse ceased coughing up blood on August 5 and enjoyed two weeks of calm. Doctor de Corniere was confident enough of her stability that he went on vacation. Unpredictably a new attack began on August 15. Thérèse suffered coughing spells, difculty in breathing, chest pains and swollen limbs. The closest doctor was Thérèse's cousin through marriage, Doctor Francis La Neele. He rushed from Caen when the Carmelites of Lisieux called him. Doctor La Neele was the rst to identify Thérèse's illness as *tuberculosis*. He reported that she was breathing with only half a lung and that the disease was now attacking her intestines. Thérèse's pain was unbearable. She described it as being stretched out on "iron spikes." When told of the fear that gangrene was setting in, Thérèse replied: "Well, all the better! While I am at it I may as well suffer very much and all over, and even have several sicknesses at the same time!" *(Conversations)* As she lie in pain, she apologized for crying out in agony. "What a grace it is to have faith," she whispered. "If I had no faith, I would have inflicted death on myself without hesitating a moment!" *(Conversations)*

Thérèse experienced peace again from the last days of August until September 13. During this time, she was cheerful and serene. She delighted the sisters who stopped briefly to see her. She even teased about the doctor's inability to help. But she knew that despite this peaceful interlude, death was near. She told Mother Agnes that she trusted "Papa God." She thanked the sisters, including her own blood sisters, who were so devoted to her. She personified a hymn of gratitude. As she lay dying, offering her sufferings for everyone throughout the world, she fulfilled her own words: "Jesus does not demand great actions from us but simply *surrender* and *gratitude*" *(Story)*.

Thérèse received communion for the last time on August 19. She offered that communion for a Carmelite ex-priest, Father Hyacinthe Loyson. Her prayers, her sufferings, her darkness, her perplexities were offered in the chalice of the Church for the good of others. "Everything I have, everything I merit is for the Church and for souls" *(Conversations)*.

Thérèse's bed had been moved to the center of the infirmary. From there she could look out of the window and enjoy the sight of the cloister garden. It was like a patch of *Les Buissonnets*. What beautiful memories she held of Papa and her sisters. She would see her father and her mother very soon. They were only days apart. Aunt and Uncle Guerin sent little treats, even a chocolate eclair, to please her. On August 30, Thérèse's bed was rolled to the entrance of the choir so she could see it for the last time. Her sister Céline, (Sister Genevieve), photographed her there. In this last photo, she is unpetaling roses over her crucifix, trying, painfully, to smile. September 8, 1897, was the seventh anniversary of her religious profession. The sisters decorated her room with a sea of flowers. Thérèse was moved at their thoughtfulness. She wanted to share her gift with the Virgin of the Smile. With great care, she wove a garland of flowers and the sisters draped it around Our Lady's neck.

Doctor de Corniere returned from vacation to find Thérèse in serious condition. Her remaining lung, also infected with tuberculosis, made breathing nearly unbearable. She was suffocating and spoke in short raspy sentences. "Mama," she said to Mother Agnes, "earth's air is denied to me. When will God grant me the air of heaven?" *(Conversations)* Thérèse's body was crucified, her emotions were shrouded in gloom; she was exhausted beyond sleep. The night was with her all the time. The feeling of emptiness led her to the border of despair. She chased the desperate thoughts from her mind. She would not give in to them. She gasped: "It is into God's arms that I'm falling" *(Conversations)*.

The days of September crept by. On the 29, Thérèse's breathing grew even more labored. After the doctor's visit, she asked Mother de Gonzague: "Is it today, Mother?" The prioress answered softly: "Yes, my child." Thérèse lingered the rest of that day and spent one more painful night. She received the sacrament of Reconciliation and then waited peacefully for her Lord to come for her. Sister Genevieve and Sister Marie of the Sacred Heart remained at Thérèse's side during the night. Mother Agnes joined them in the morning.

On September 30, Thérèse grew worse. Around 3:00 P.M. she extended her arms in the shape of a cross. She rested one arm on Mother Agnes' shoulder, and the other on Sister Genevieve's. She wanted to be a victim of love as was her Savior. The Lord was soon to grant her the *death of love* for which she prayed. At about 4:30 in the afternoon, Mother Agnes was alone with Thérèse and became alarmed when all the color drained rapidly from her sister's face. Mother de Gonzague and the entire community returned. Thérèse smiled, but remained silent. During the next two hours the death rattle shook her. Thérèse's "face was flushed, her hands purple, and her feet were as cold as ice" (Epilogue of *Story of a Soul*). Even while she shivered, beads of perspiration covered her forehead and cheeks. She smiled at Sister Genevieve who bathed her parched lips with ice.

The Angelus bell rang at 6:00 P.M. Thérèse gazed at the statue of the Virgin of the Smile. She clutched her crucifix. The infirmary was tranquil. The sisters, who had been there two hours, quietly slipped away. Thérèse spoke briefly with Mother de Gonzague. Then she rested her head on the pillow, turning her face toward the right. The prioress acted quickly. She had the monastery bell rung, summoning the nuns back to the room. As the community knelt, Thérèse, her eyes riveted to her crucifix, exclaimed: "Oh! I love him!" "My God, I love you!" *(Conversations)* Her eyes lifted and focused slightly above the Virgin's statue. She seemed to be immersed in joy. Her complexion became radiant with a healthy glow. Then she closed her eyes peacefully and died. It was 7:20 P.M., Thursday, September 30, 1897.

Thérèse was waked in the choir until Sunday evening. Her funeral Mass was celebrated in the convent chapel and she was buried in the Lisieux cemetery the next day, Monday, October 4. What appeared to be the end of her short, seemingly uneventful life was really just the beginning....

Thérèse lying outside the cloister infirmary, August 30, 1897.

16

Just the Beginning

On March 7, 1898, Bishop Hugonin gave his permission for Thérèse's *Story of a Soul* to be published. From 1899 pilgrims began to flock to her grave to pray. Thérèse's cause for sainthood was presented to Rome by the Carmelites on July 9, 1906. Letters about favors received through her intercession poured into the Carmel of Lisieux. In 1910 alone, the nuns received 9,741 such letters from France and beyond. Devotion to Thérèse continued to spread. On August 14, 1921, Pope Benedict XV officially began the investigation of the sanctity of her life. At the ceremony the pope delivered a moving homily on the importance of Thérèse's way of *spiritual childhood*.

On April 29, 1923, Pope Pius XI declared Thérèse "Blessed," calling her "the star of his pontificate." The same pope canonized her a saint on May 17, 1925. On December 14, 1927, Pope Pius XI named Thérèse *patron of the missions,* along with St. Francis Xavier.

Most recently, on Mission Sunday, October 19, 1997, Pope John Paul II proclaimed Thérèse a *Doctor of the Church.* She is the youngest person to have received this honor and the third woman to join the ranks of the Doctors, following after St. Catherine of Siena and St. Teresa of Avila.

If Thérèse's life could be summed up in one word it would have to be *love*, a love that sprang from her unshakable confidence in the goodness and mercy of God, a love that penetrated beyond all boundaries—even those of death. Thérèse has promised, "If God answers my desires, my heaven will be spent on earth until the end of the world. Yes, I want to spend my heaven in doing good on earth" *(Conversations)*.

Thérèse continues to love.

Prayers in Honor of St. Thérèse

A Prayer to Obtain the Spirit of St. Thérèse

O God of Merciful Love, you have never failed your people in any age, but have always raised up saints as lamps to their feet on the road to salvation. We thank you for the waterfall of grace you poured down on St. Thérèse of Lisieux. Because she really believed the Gospel she understood it, and you have endowed her with the gift of unfolding its riches for us in our own day. For this we thank you most sincerely, and we ask for the perseverance to follow "the little way" of holiness that you yourself revealed to her.

Teach us to give up our unrealistic dreams of heroism and settle down to the task of being ourselves and accepting what we are. Help us want your will and nothing else—nothing at all, Lord. Help us find it in the real world of every day's here and now. Convince us that the present moment with its light and its darkness, its highs and its lows, its joys and its sorrows, is nothing else than your own dwelling place, your very temple into which you call us to be loved and to love, to love you and to love our brothers and sisters . . . and not least of all to love our own poor wonderful selves.

We ask this through your own dear Son, our Lord Jesus, who lives and reigns with you in the joyous embrace of the Holy Spirit, one God for always and forever. Amen.

© Bishop Patrick V. Ahern, D.D.

Prayer of St. Thérèse of Lisieux to Know God's Will

Lord grant that I may always allow myself to be guided by you, always follow your plans, and perfectly accomplish your holy will.

Grant that in all things, great and small, today and all the days of my life, I may do whatever you may require of me. Help me to respond to the slightest prompting of your grace, so that I may be your trustworthy instrument. May your will be done in time and eternity, by me, in me, and through me. Amen.

© Hermitage Designs, Eureka Springs, AR

My Novena Rose Prayer

O little Thérèse of the Child Jesus,
please pick for me a rose
from the heavenly gardens and
send it to me as a message of love.
O Little Flower of Jesus,
ask God today to grant the favors I now place
with confidence in your hands....
(Mention specific request)
St. Thérèse, help me to always believe as you did,
in God's great love for me,
so that I might imitate your "little way" each day.
Amen.

© Society of the Little Flower, Darien, IL

Miraculous Prayer to St. Thérèse

O glorious St. Thérèse, whom almighty God has raised up to help and inspire the human family, I beg your miraculous intercession. You are so powerful in obtaining every need of body and spirit from the heart of God. Holy Mother Church proclaims you "prodigy of miracles ... the greatest saint of modern times." Now I fervently beseech you to answer my petition (mention here) and to carry out your promises of *spending heaven doing good upon earth ... of letting fall from heaven a shower of roses.* Little Flower, give me your childlike faith, to see the face of God in the people and experiences of my life, and to love God with full confidence. St. Thérèse of the Child Jesus, I will fulfill your plea "to be made known everywhere" and I will continue to lead others to Jesus through you. Amen.

© Society of the Little Flower, Darien, IL

Novena Prayer for Vocations

St. Thérèse, you answered the Lord's call to become love in the heart of the Church by entering Carmel and living the hidden life of contemplative prayer, fasting, and self-offering for the missions of the Church and the salvation of souls. Through your intercession, hear our prayers for an increase in vocations to the priesthood and religious life in our diocese. Send us laborers for our vineyard who will be true apostles of the Lord, faithful to the service of his truth, the pursuit of holiness, and always sensitive to the needs of others before their own. We ask this through Christ our Lord. Amen.

St. Thérèse, patroness of seminarians, pray for us.

© Society of the Little Flower, Darien, IL

Prayer to Learn the "Little Way" of St. Thérèse

Lord Jesus, through the life of St. Thérèse with its lesson of trust and simplicity, you have brought new hope to all who long to open their hearts to you in prayer. Teach us the secret of her "Little Way" and help us to understand that it is not in long prayers of lofty words that we must talk with you. Rather, it is in the deep love with which we bring you our gratitude, our smiles and our tears. Amen.

© Monastery of St. Joseph, Discalced Carmelites, Terre Haute, IN

Stay with Us, Jesus

Abide with us, Jesus, in the midst of our busy hours. When we are tempted, discouraged or burdened in any way, may we, with a silent cry of our hearts, turn to you in loving trust. Transform each passing moment of time into an eternal moment of prayer. And Good Jesus, from your overflowing mercy, fill every troubled human heart with the confident faith of St. Thérèse. In joy, in sorrow, in every circumstance, may our hearts rest in your infinite peace. Amen.

© Monastery of St. Joseph, Discalced Carmelites, Terre Haute, IN

O Eternal Father

O Eternal Father, whose infinite love watches in wisdom over each day of my life, grant me the light to see in sorrow as in joy, in trial as in peace, in uncertainty as in confidence, the way your divine providence has marked for me. Give me that faith and trust in your care for me, so pleasing to you in St. Thérèse of the Child Jesus and I will walk in darkness as in light, holding your hand and finding in all the blessings I receive from your loving bounty, that "Everything is a grace." Amen.

© by Sister Teresa of the Trinity Hewitt, Monastery of St. Joseph, Discalced Carmelites, Terre Haute, IN

With Empty Hands

I come before you with empty hands.
All the secret store of grace I fling into needy hearts,
crying in the bitter night of fear and loneliness.
Spendthrift of your Love, I keep before me
your empty hands—
empty and riven with the great nails
hollowing out rivers of mercy,
until all your substance was poured out.
So I, my Jesus, with hands emptied for your love,
stand confident before your cross,
love's crimson emblem.
It is the empty who are filled:
those who have made themselves
spendthrifts for you alone fill the least of your brethren
while they themselves are nourished by your love...
more and more emptied that
they may be filled with you.

© by Sister Teresa of the Trinity Hewitt, Monastery of St. Joseph, Discalced Carmelites, Terre Haute, IN

A Prayer for Trust and Acceptance

St. Thérèse, in your brief life on earth, a life of single-heartedness and trust, your prayer and your deeds reflected the prayer and deeds of Jesus. You glimpsed his face only in shadowed sorrow, but your heart was ever turned in bright hope to the brilliance of the eternal homeland.

The acceptance of your littleness was your hidden greatness; your weakness was your power, and your cross was your joy. Help us, Thérèse, to learn that for us also, the way of total surrender is the only way to know and to see the face of Jesus.

Upon your brow in death, there shone the beauty of peace, the serenity of simplicity, and the transparency of faith—etched by Jesus, as your glimpse in saddened sorrow became the clear gaze of radiant vision in the Homeland of unchanging Love. Amen.

© Sister Joseph of Jesus Mary Mckenzie, Monastery of St. Joseph, Discalced Carmelites, Terre Haute, IN

Only Jesus

Jesus,
touch us,
teach us,
change us,
as you did St. Thérèse,
that we may carry
your Gospel in our hands,
cherish it in our hearts,
breathe it in our lives,
make all our prayer,
all our service
only Jesus.

© Sister Joseph of Jesus Mary Mckenzie, Monastery of St. Joseph, Discalced Carmelites, Terre Haute, IN

For Further Reading

Autobiography of a Saint. Translated by Ronald Knox. London: Fount Classics, a division of Harper-Collins Publishers, 1958.

Complete Spiritual Doctrine of St. Thérèse of Lisieux. Translated by Walter Van De Putte. New York: Alba House, 1961.

Happiness of God, The by Susan Leslie. Middlegreen, Slough, England: St. Paul Publications, 1988.

Hinds' Feet on High Places by Hannah Hurnard. Wheaton, Ill: Living Books, Tyndale House Publishers, Inc., 1975, 1986.

I Believe in Love by Pere Jean du Coeur de Jesus d'Elbee. Petersham, Massachusetts: St. Bede Publications, 1974.

Louis Martin Father of a Saint by Dr. Joyce R. Emert, OCDS. Staten Island, New York: Alba House, 1983.

Photo Album of Saint Thérèse of Lisieux. Commentary by Francois de Saint-Marie, O.C.D. Translated by Peter-Thomas Rohrbach, O.C.D. Allen, Texas: Christian Classics, 1995.

Poetry of St. Thérèse of Lisieux, The. Translated by Donald Kinney, O.C.D. Washington, D.C.: ICS Publications, 1996.

Praying with Thérèse of Lisieux by Joseph F. Schmidt, FSC. Winona, Minnesota: St. Mary's Press, 1995.

Saint Thérèse of Lisieux by Monsignor Guy Gaucher. Strasbourg, France: Editions Du Signe, 1994.

Spiritual Childhood by Vernon Johnson. Kansas City: Sheed and Ward, 1984.

Spiritual Genius of Saint Thérèse of Lisieux by Jean Guitton. Translated by Felicity Lang. Liguori, Mo: Triumph Books, 1997.

St. Thérèse of Lisieux—A TRIDUUM, tapes by Bishop Patrick V. Ahern. Canfield, Ohio: Alba House Cassettes.

St. Thérèse of Lisieux by Those Who Knew Her. Translated by Christopher O'Mahoney. Dublin, Ireland: Veritas Publications, 1975.

St. Thérèse of Lisieux. General Correspondence, Volumes 1 and 2. Washington, D.C.: ICS Publications, 1982, 1988.

St. Thérèse of Lisieux: Her Last Conversations. Translated by Rev. John Clarke, O.C.D. Washington, D.C.: ICS Publications, 1977.

St. Theresa the Little Flower by Sr. Gesualda of the Holy Spirit. Boston, Massachusetts: Pauline Books & Media, 1960.

Storm of Glory by John Beevers. New York: Image-Doubleday, Inc., 1949.

Story of a Life, The: St. Thérèse of Lisieux by Guy Gaucher, O.C.D. San Francisco: Harper Collins, 1993.

Story of a Soul (Autobiography of St. Thérèse of Lisieux), Third Edition. Translated from the original manuscripts by Rev. John Clarke, O.C.D. Washington, D.C.: ICS Publications, 1996.

Thérèse by Dorothy Day. Springfield, Ill.: Templegate, 1985.

Thérèse: An Intimate Companion, audio tapes by Bishop Patrick V. Ahern. Canfield, Ohio: Alba House Communications.

Thérèse and Lisieux by Helmuth Nils Loose and Pierre Descouvemont. Grand Rapids, MI: Wm B. Eerdmans (in conjunction with *Novalis* and *Veritas* Publications), 1996.

Thérèse of Lisieux: A Vocation of Love by Marie-Pascal Ducrocq. Staten Island, New York: Alba House, 1982.

Thérèse of Lisieux: The Story of a Mission by Hans Urs Von Balthasar. New York: Sheed and Ward, 1954.

Under the Torrent of His Love: Thérèse of Lisieux, a Spiritual Genius by Father Marie-Eugene of the Child Jesus. Staten Island, New York: Alba House, 1995.

BOOKS & MEDIA

The Daughters of St. Paul operate book and media centers at the following addresses. Visit, call or write the one nearest you today, or find us on the World Wide Web, www.pauline.org

CALIFORNIA
   3908 Sepulveda Blvd., Culver City, CA 90230; 310-397-8676
   5945 Balboa Ave., San Diego, CA 92111; 858-565-9181
   46 Geary Street, San Francisco, CA 94108; 415-781-5180

FLORIDA
   145 S.W. 107th Ave., Miami, FL 33174; 305-559-6715

HAWAII
   1143 Bishop Street, Honolulu, HI 96813; 808-521-2731
   Neighbor Islands call: 800-259-8463

ILLINOIS
   172 North Michigan Ave., Chicago, IL 60601; 312-346-4228

LOUISIANA
   4403 Veterans Memorial Blvd., Metairie, LA 70006; 504-887-7631

MASSACHUSETTS
   Rte. 1, 885 Providence Hwy., Dedham, MA 02026; 781-326-5385

MISSOURI
   9804 Watson Rd., St. Louis, MO 63126; 314-965-3512

NEW JERSEY
   561 U.S. Route 1, Wick Plaza, Edison, NJ 08817; 732-572-1200

NEW YORK
   150 East 52nd Street, New York, NY 10022; 212-754-1110
   78 Fort Place, Staten Island, NY 10301; 718-447-5071

OHIO
   2105 Ontario Street, Cleveland, OH 44115; 216-621-9427

PENNSYLVANIA
   9171-A Roosevelt Blvd., Philadelphia, PA 19114; 215-676-9494

SOUTH CAROLINA
   243 King Street, Charleston, SC 29401; 843-577-0175

TENNESSEE
   4811 Poplar Ave., Memphis, TN 38117; 901-761-2987

TEXAS
   114 Main Plaza, San Antonio, TX 78205; 210-224-8101

VIRGINIA
   1025 King Street, Alexandria, VA 22314; 703-549-3806

CANADA
   3022 Dufferin Street, Toronto, Ontario, Canada M6B 3T5; 416-781-9131
   1155 Yonge Street, Toronto, Ontario, Canada M4T 1W2; 416-934-3440

¡También somos su fuente para libros, videos y música en español!